Better Cookery for diabetics

Over 130 delicious and healthy recipes for diabetics,

their families and friends to enjoy.

Compiled by Jill Metcalfe,

dietitian at the British Diabetic Association

Acknowledgements

The British Diabetic Association thanks Mrs Helen Blerkom, Mrs Celia Norman and their Home Economics students at the Department of Food Sciences, Polytechnic of North London, for their help in compiling this recipe book.

Thanks also to Harrods for help with accessories and Record Pasta for samples of their goods for the photographs.

Editing and production by Jennifer Dyer
Photography by John Melville
Printed 1981
Reprinted 1983, 1985
© British Diabetic Association
Printed by Burgess & Son (Abingdon) Ltd.,
Abingdon, Oxfordshire

British Diabetic Association

THE BRITISH DIABETIC ASSOCIATION has been working for diabetics for over 50 years. Our aims are simply to help diabetics of all ages and to defeat diabetes through research.

For the young we run an extensive youth programme including educational holidays for diabetic children and teenagers and parent/child weekends.

For the elderly insulin-dependent diabetic, we organise holidays. For all members we provide free guidance and help on social, welfare and dietetic questions – but not on individual treatment. We have over 300 branches which hold regular meetings.

As a member, you are sent the bi-monthly magazine BALANCE free. This gives you news of progress in medical care and research, news about diets, recipes and personalities and practical hints on day-to-day problems.

The Association depends entirely on voluntary support from people like you.

Subscription rates:
Life Membership: a single payment of £105 or seven-year covenant of £15.
Full Membership: £5 per year.
Pensioner Membership (old aged, widows, disabled or unemployed): £1.00 per year.

To become a member fill in the application form on the right and send it with your subscription to:
British Diabetic Association,
10 Queen Anne Street, London, W1M 0BD.
Our telephone number is: 01-323 1531.

Join the BDA
- **to help yourself**
- **to help other sufferers**
- **to help find a cure**

To: The Secretary General,
British Diabetic Association,
10 Queen Anne Street,
London W1M 0BD

Please enrol me as a member of the British Diabetic Association for which I enclose the sum of:

£

(Use Block Letters please)

Surname . . . .

First Name . . . .

Address . . . .

. . . .

Date of Birth . . . . **Occupation** . . . .
(This information will be treated as strictly confidential)

Date . . . . **Signature** . . . .

British Diabetic Association – A Company Limited by Guarantee
Registered Office – 10 Queen Anne Street, London W1M 0BD
Registered in England Registration No. 339181

Contents

Illustrations

The Aim of this Recipe Book

The aim of this recipe book is to show that interesting and well-balanced meals can be enjoyed by diabetics and their families and friends. There is no need for diabetics to eat "special foods" or watch while members of their families sit down and enjoy different meals. New dietary recommendations now emphasise the importance of a carefully balanced diet for all the family and not just the diabetic.

All the ingredients used in these recipes are normal, everyday foods. The only difference is that if sweetness is required, an alternative to sugar has been used. Wholemeal flour and pasta and brown rice may not previously have been used but their delicious taste and benefits to the health of the family will hopefully encourage many more people to include these foods in their meals.

Why

Research strongly suggests that a diet high in natural fibre-containing foods and containing little fat, can improve long term health prospects. For the diabetic, a high fibre diet has the added advantage of appearing to reduce the sharp rise in blood sugar that can occur after meals. High fibre foods are often found to be more filling and satisfying than their refined counterparts. This is an advantage to diabetics (and others) who have to watch their weight.

The need to reduce the amount of fat and fatty foods in the diet has been recognised throughout the developed world.

The British Diabetic Association, with the help of the country's leading experts on diabetic care, has recognised the need to educate the public about this new dietary approach. *Better Cookery for diabetics* gives practical ideas on how to change to this healthier way of eating and the BDA hopes that by using this recipe book diabetics and their families will enjoy delicious and healthy meals.

Using this recipe book

All the recipes in this book have been fully tested and are easy to follow but please take note of the following:

Servings and values

At the end of each recipe the number of servings which can be obtained from the specified ingredients, is indicated. These are based on average serving sizes but as appetites vary, a recipe for four could also be suitable for three or five depending on circumstances.

Total carbohydrate (CHO) and calorie values have therefore been given in bold type on the bottom right of each page, except when individual helpings are available, eg one pasty, one sausage roll etc.

To calculate the carbohydrate or calorie value of each serving:

Divide the carbohydrate and calorie total by the number of servings obtained from the recipe. This will give the amount of carbohydrate or number of calories in each portion.

eg Tuna Flan has a total of 80g carbohydrate (CHO) and 1660 calories.

If the Flan is divided into four equal servings each portion would contain 20g carbohydrate (CHO) and 415 calories (80g CHO ÷ 4 = 20g CHO; 1660 calories ÷ 4 = 415 calories).

If the flan was divided into six smaller servings each portion would contain 13g CHO (80 ÷ 6) and 275 calories (1660 ÷ 6).

Weights & Measures

These recipes will give successful results whether you choose to use imperial or metric measures. Keep to one or the other in a recipe as the conversion is not exact and the recipe will not work if you keep swapping them.

Use these conversion tables for easy reference. Please note that there are sometimes "jumps" in the chart — these are necessary to make the conversion more accurate. All the carbohydrate and calorie calculations have been made on the metric recipes and for the greatest accuracy the metric system should be used.

Weights

25 g	1 oz
50 g	2 oz
75 g	3 oz
100 g	4 oz
150 g	5 oz
175 g	6 oz
200 g	7 oz
225 g	8 oz
250 g	9 oz
275 g	10 oz
300 g	11 oz
350 g	12 oz
375 g	13 oz
400 g	14 oz
425 g	15 oz
450 g	16 oz

Measuring Spoons

1 × 2.5 ml sp	½ tsp
1 × 5 ml sp	1 tsp
1 × 10 ml sp	1 dsp
1 × 15 ml sp	1 tblsp

Oven Temperatures

Gas	Centigrade	Fahrenheit
No 2	150°	300°
No 3	160°	325°
No 4	180°	350°
No 5	190°	375°
No 6	200°	400°
No 7	220°	425°
No 8	230°	450°
No 9	240°	475°

Sizes

2½ cm	1 in
5 cm	2 ins
7½ cm	3 ins
10 cm	4 ins
13 cm	5 ins
15 cm	6 ins
18 cm	7 ins
20 cm	8 ins
23 cm	9 ins
26 cm	10 ins
28 cm	11 ins
30½ cm	12 ins

Liquid Measures

150 ml	¼ pt
275 ml	½ pt
425 ml	¾ pt
550 ml	1 pt

Soups & Sauces

Soup

A warming bowl of soup when served with wholemeal bread or rolls can be a meal in itself. Use these recipes as a guide then develop your own favourites using dried beans and peas for interest and colour. If you do not have a liquidiser use a balloon whisk instead.

Sauces

Sauces can add variety and flavour to the dullest meal — but traditional recipes are low in fibre and high in fat and calories. A wholemeal sauce with different flavourings is healthier and tastier for the whole family.

(right) Quick Tomato Soup

Cheesy Wheat Soup

A thick, nourishing soup, suitable for cold winter days.

75 g/3 oz wholewheat grains
1100 ml/2 pt vegetable stock
25 g/1 oz ground millet
salt and pepper
1 × 5 ml sp/1 tsp mixed herbs
pinch of cayenne pepper
1 onion, chopped
50 g/2 oz mushrooms, chopped
2 tomatoes, skinned and chopped
1 × 15 ml sp/1 tblsp vegetable oil
225 g/8 oz cottage cheese }
25 g/1 oz chives } mixed, *or*
225 g/8 oz cottage cheese with chives
(pre-mixed)

Wash and dry wheat and grind in a liquidiser. Place stock in large pan and bring to the boil. Add wheat, ground millet, herbs, cayenne pepper and season well. Cook (stirring occasionally) for 30-40 minutes until wheat is tender. Fry onion, mushroom and tomato in the oil until soft. Add this mixture to the wheat mixture and stir. Add half the cottage cheese to the saucepan and cook for a further 10 minutes. Season to taste. Pour into a soup tureen and float the remaining cottage cheese on top.

Serves 8-10

80g CHO
640 Calories } total

Chicken & Rice Soup

1100 ml/2 pt chicken stock
1 medium onion, chopped
4 carrots, sliced
2 sticks celery, chopped
1 × 2.5 ml sp/½ tsp salt
1 × 2.5 ml sp/½ tsp pepper
50 g/2 oz brown rice
2 bayleaves
100 g/4 oz cooked chicken, sliced
parsley to garnish

Place chicken stock, vegetables, salt and pepper in pan and cook gently until vegetables are tender. Remove vegetables from stock and set aside. Add rice and bayleaves to stock and simmer for 30-40 minutes until cooked. Discard bayleaves. Purée the vegetables in a blender then add with chicken to the stock and simmer for a further 5 minutes.
Garnish with chopped parsley.

Serves 6

60g CHO
400 Calories } total

Chick-pea Soup

2 medium onions, chopped
1 red pepper, de-seeded and chopped
1 green pepper, de-seeded and chopped
5 sticks celery, chopped
2 × 15 ml sp/2 tblsp olive or vegetable oil
1 clove garlic, crushed
1 bayleaf
225 g/8 oz chick-peas, soaked overnight
825 ml/1½ pt chicken stock
100 g/4 oz salami, thinly sliced
    and chopped
salt and pepper

Fry onions, peppers and celery over a low heat, until softened. Add garlic and bayleaf, then 1 minute later add chick-peas and chicken stock. Simmer for 1½ hours or until chick-peas are tender. Remove ½ cup of the peas, liquidise, return to the soup. Add chopped salami, season well and simmer for a further 10 minutes.

Serves 6

120g CHO
1600 Calories } total

Quick Tomato Soup

3 large tomatoes, skinned and chopped
2 onions, grated or finely diced
550 ml/1 pt tomato juice
275 ml/½ pt stock
salt and pepper
1 × 2.5 ml sp/½ tsp dried thyme
1 × 5 ml sp/1 tsp dried parsley
25 g/1 oz fresh wholemeal breadcrumbs,
    toasted

Place all ingredients, except breadcrumbs, in a pan and season well. Bring to the boil and simmer for 8-10 minutes. Pour into serving dishes and sprinkle with the toasted breadcrumbs.

Serves 4-6

20g CHO
180 Calories } **total**

*Illustrated

Vegetable & Rice Soup

3 rashers bacon, de-rinded and chopped
1 leek, chopped
2 sticks celery, chopped
¼ cabbage, shredded
2 carrots, chopped
100 g/4 oz pearl barley
100 g/4 oz frozen peas
1 × 15 ml sp/1 tblsp tomato purée
100 g/4 oz brown rice
825 ml/1½ pt brown stock
1 × 5 ml sp/1 tsp rosemary
1 × 5 ml sp/1 tsp tarragon
salt and pepper

Gently cook bacon (without added fat) in a heavy saucepan. Drain off excess fat, add fresh vegetables. Sauté for 10 minutes or until vegetables just start to soften. Add remaining ingredients. Bring to the boil, season well, then simmer for 1 hour.

Serves 6

180g CHO
1000 Calories } total

Wholemeal Sauces

Tasty alternatives to white sauce.

Basic sauce:
25 g/1 oz wholemeal flour
25 g/1 oz low fat margarine
275 ml/½ pt skimmed milk
seasoning
mixed herbs (optional)

For variety add one of the following:
25 g/1 oz hard cheese, grated
50 g/2 oz cottage cheese
100 g/4 oz mushrooms, washed and thinly
   sliced
100 g/4 oz onions, finely chopped
1 × 15 ml sp/1 tblsp tomato purée
1 × 10 ml sp/1 dssp curry powder and
   1 beaten egg

Melt fat, stir in flour, cook for 2 minutes stirring continually. Remove from heat, add skimmed milk and herbs gradually, stirring well. Return to heat, bring to boil and cook for 2-3 minutes. Season to taste.
Use the sauce to coat or accompany vegetables or as an addition to meat and fish.
Makes 275 ml/ ½ pt sauce.

30g CHO } **Basic sauce**
270 Calories } **total**

Pizzas & Pastries

This section proves that foods made with wholemeal flour and less fat than usual can be just as delicious as their conventional counterparts. The fat content of pastry can never be greatly reduced as it is not possible to use a low fat margarine successfully. As a result the recipes in this section are still high in fat and calories. Use them carefully and not often, always serving low fat, low calorie accompaniments or salads.

(left) Frankfurter Pizza, Mixed Grill Flan, Tuna Flan

Cheese Pizzas

Dough:
25 g/1 oz yeast
275/½ pt lukewarm water
225 g/8 oz strong plain flour ⎫
225 g/8 oz wholemeal flour ⎬ sieved together
1 × 2.5 ml sp/½ tsp salt ⎭

Topping:
50 g/2 oz cheddar cheese
50 g/2 oz wholemeal breadcrumbs
225 g/8 oz can tomatoes
1 small red pepper, de-seeded and diced
1 small green pepper, de-seeded and diced
1 medium onion, chopped
100 g/4 oz lean back bacon,
    cut in long strips
100 g/4 oz mushrooms, sliced

Dissolve yeast in water, mix with flour and knead to a smooth dough. Leave to rise until double in size. Knead again for 3-4 minutes, shape into 6 equal flat rounds and leave to prove for 10 minutes.

Mix grated cheese and breadcrumbs together. Cover dough with tomatoes, sprinkle with cheese and breadcrumb mixture. Add peppers and onion. Make a lattice with bacon slices and place a slice of mushroom in each space. (Can be frozen at this stage).

Bake in oven at No 7/220°C/425°F for 20-30 minutes or until dough is well risen and crisp on the bottom.

Serve with fresh green salad.

Serves 6

55g CHO ⎫
330 Calories ⎬ each
                  ⎭

Frankfurter Pizza

A quick pizza using a pastry base.

Base:
75 g/3 oz self-raising flour
1 × 2.5 ml sp/½ tsp salt
75 g/3 oz wholemeal flour
50 g/2 oz vegetable fat
water to bind

Topping:
25 g/1 oz low fat margarine
1 small onion, chopped
100 g/4 oz mushrooms, sliced
10 frankfurters, sliced
50 g/2 oz tomato purée
1 small can sweetcorn
1 small can kidney beans, drained
½ green pepper, chopped
salt and pepper

Rub fat into the flour and salt. Add enough water until mixture resembles a firm dough. Shape into 23 cm/9" round and place on a greased baking sheet. Meanwhile melt margarine and cook onion gently until soft. Add remaining ingredients and cook gently for 10 minutes. Spoon on to the base leaving about 2.5 cm/1" around the edge. Bake at No 7/220°C/425°F for 15-20 minutes or until the base is crisp.
The base can be pre-cooked and the topping added just before serving if preferred.

Serves 4-6

*Illustrated

180g CHO
1400 Calories } **total**

Mince Pies

Pastry:
175 g/6 oz wholemeal flour
75 g/3 oz margarine
cold water to bind

Filling:
1 medium cooking apple
1 large carrot
25 g/1 oz currants
25 g/1 oz sultanas
25 g/1 oz walnuts
1 × 5 ml sp/1 tsp mixed spice
juice of 1 lemon
1 × 10 ml sp/1 dssp low fat margarine

Peel apple and carrot. Finely chop dry ingredients or liquidise for approximately ½ minute. Add juice, spice and margarine. Mix well. Cover, leave to stand for 24 hours. Make pastry. Rest in fridge for 24 hours. Roll out pastry thinly. Cut out 15 bases and 15 tops using a fluted pastry cutter. Place bases in greased tins and fill with mincemeat.
Cover with tops. Press edges together and brush with a little egg and milk. Bake at No 5/190°C/375°F until golden brown.
Cool on a wire rack.

10g CHO
100 Calories } **each**

Mixed Grill Flan

Pastry:
100 g/4 oz wholemeal flour
50 g/2 oz margarine
3 × 15 ml sp/3 tblsp water

Filling:
225 g/8 oz lambs kidney, quartered and cored
50 g/2 oz bacon, chopped
100 g/4 oz mushrooms, chopped
1 medium onion, chopped
1 small can kidney beans, finely chopped
1 × 15 ml/1 tblsp wholemeal flour
150 ml/¼ pt stock

Topping:
1 × 15 ml sp/1 tblsp chopped parsley
2 small tomatoes, sliced

Rub fat into flour. Add enough water to form a moderately soft dough. Roll out and line 20 cm/ 8" flan ring and bake blind at No 5/190°C/ 375°F for approximately 25 minutes or until pastry is dry and crisp.

Fry the bacon without added fat. Add the kidney, onion, mushrooms and kidney beans. When kidney is cooked add flour and gradually add stock. Bring to the boil stirring all the time (this mixture should be fairly thick). Spoon mixture into the cooked flan case. Place in oven for 10 minutes. Garnish with chopped parsley and tomatoes.

Serves 4

120g CHO
1400 Calories } total

*Illustrated

Quick Chicken Pizza

Base:
275 g/10 oz packet brown bread mix

Topping:
1 × 10 ml sp/1 dssp low fat margarine
150 g/5 oz onions, chopped
425 g/15 oz can tomatoes
1 × 10 ml sp/1 dssp oregano
275 g/10 oz cooked chicken, cut into
    small pieces
salt and pepper
75 g/3 oz grated Edam cheese

Melt margarine and gently cook chopped onions for 5 minutes. Add tomatoes and oregano and boil until quantity is reduced by half. Add chicken and season to taste. Simmer on a low heat until remaining liquid has evaporated, to leave a thick consistency.

Prepare breadmix base as instructed on packet. Roll out dough into a circle 26 cm/10" in diameter. Place on a baking sheet and cover with the topping. Sprinkle with the grated cheese and cook for 20-30 minutes at No 6/200°C/400°F or until dough is well risen and golden brown.

Serves 4

180g CHO
1600 Calories } total

Sausage Rolls

Pastry:
150 g/5 oz wholemeal flour
50 g/2 oz soft margarine
25 g/1 oz vegetable fat
pinch of salt

Filling:
225 g/8 oz good quality pork sausagemeat
1 × 10 ml sp/1 dssp dried mixed herbs
seasoning

Sift flour and salt, rub in fat. Add enough cold water to bind. Form into a ball and rest in fridge for 30 minutes. Meanwhile mix sausagemeat, herbs and seasoning together. Rest in fridge. Roll out pastry on lightly floured board and form 12 sausage rolls. Brush with egg and milk. Rest for 10 minutes in fridge before baking at No 6/200°C/400°F until golden brown.

10g CHO
150 Calories } **each**

Steak & Kidney Pie

Shortcrust pastry:
100 g/4 oz wholemeal flour
100 g/4 oz plain flour
100 g/4 oz margarine
2-3 × 15 ml sp/2-3 tblsp water
pinch of salt

Filling:
2 onions, sliced
900 g/2 lb lean stewing steak,
    cut into 2.5 cm/1" cubes
225 g/8 oz kidney, cut into 1.25 cm/½"
    pieces
50 g/2 oz wholemeal flour
275 ml/½ pt beef stock
1 × 2.5 ml sp/½ tsp dried marjoram
1 bayleaf
salt and pepper

Toss steak and kidney in flour, seal in a hot pan. Add onions. Stir in any excess flour and gradually add stock, marjoram, bayleaf and seasoning. Bring to the boil, stirring all the time. Cover, reduce heat and simmer for 1-2 hours or until the meat is tender. Rub fat into flour until it resembles fine breadcrumbs, add enough water to form a soft dough and leave wrapped in the refrigerator for 30 minutes. Transfer meat to an ovenproof dish, cover with the rolled out pastry. Make a small hole in the centre, and brush with skimmed milk. Bake at No 5/190°C/375°F for 45 minutes to 1 hour or until the pastry is crisp.

Serves 8

180g CHO
3200 Calories } total

Tuna Flan

Pastry:
100 g/4 oz wholemeal flour
50 g/2 oz margarine
3 × 15 ml sp/3 tblsp water

Filling:
25 g/1 oz low fat margarine
1 × 15 ml sp/1 tblsp wholemeal flour
275 ml/½ pt skimmed milk
50 g/2 oz mature cheddar cheese, grated
200 g/7 oz tuna (in brine), flaked
salt and pepper
extra grated cheese, optional
pinch of cayenne pepper, optional

Rub fat into flour, add enough water to form a firm dough. Roll out and line a 20 cm/8" flan ring. Bake blind at No 5/190°C/375°F for 25 minutes or until pastry is dry and crisp. Meanwhile melt fat, stir in flour, cook for 2-3 minutes. Remove from the heat and gradually add milk. Bring to the boil stirring all the time and cook for a further 2 minutes. Add cheese and tuna, season well. Pour mixture into pastry case and sprinkle a little cheese over the top if desired. Brown under the grill. Sprinkle with cayenne pepper before serving.

Serves 4-6

*Illustrated

80g CHO
1660 Calories } total

Wholewheat Pasties

Pastry:
275 g/10 oz wholemeal flour
pinch of salt
150 g/5 oz mixture margarine/vegetable fat
2-3 × 15 ml sp/2-3 tblsp cold water

Filling:
350 g/12 oz mince, cooked and drained
    of fat
100 g/4 oz parsnips or turnips, cooked
    and diced
100 g/4 oz carrots, cooked and diced
1 × 5 ml sp/1 tsp Worcester sauce
salt and pepper
1 egg, beaten

Sift flour and salt into bowl, rub in fat until mixture resembles fine breadcrumbs. Add just enough water to form a soft dough. Leave wrapped in the refrigerator for 20 minutes. Mix vegetables and mince with Worcester sauce and season well. Roll out pastry and cut four rounds, approximately 20 cm/8" in diameter. Place ¼ of the filling in middle of each round, dampen the edges with water and draw the sides up on top, seal well and crimp the join. Prick lightly with a fork, glaze with beaten egg. Bake at No 7/220°C/ 425°F for 25 minutes or until golden brown.

Serves 4

50g CHO
700 Calories } **each**

Beef & Lamb

The recipes in this section use only small amounts of low fat margarine. Remember to trim all fat off meat and drain fat from frying pans or pots wherever indicated. Vegetables, (fresh, frozen, dried or canned) have been used to extend the meat portions. Apart from cutting costs, the use of these vegetables is particularly helpful for diabetics as these foods are less likely to cause rapid rises in blood sugar after eating.

(left) Quick Chilli Con Carne, Savoury Burgers, Curried Lamb and Chapattis

35

Beef & Lentil Stew

A hearty stew topped with wholemeal scones.

Stew:
1 × 15 ml sp/1 tblsp vegetable oil
450 g/1 lb lean stewing steak, cubed
350 g/12 oz onions, sliced
225 g/8 oz carrots, sliced
175 g/6 oz lentils, rinsed and drained
550 ml/1 pt dark stock
salt and pepper

Scones:
100 g/4 oz plain flour
100 g/4 oz wholemeal flour
1 × 5 ml sp/1 tsp bicarbonate of soda
1 × 5 ml sp/1 tsp cream of tartar
50 g/2 oz margarine
1 large egg, beaten
150 ml/¼ pt skimmed milk
pinch of salt

Stew: sauté trimmed meat and onions in oil until brown, drain. Add carrots, lentils and stock and season well. Place in ovenproof dish and cook at No 3/160°C/325°F for 2½-3 hours, or cook in a pressure cooker for 30 minutes at 15 lb pressure. If too thick add an additional 150 ml/¼ pt beef stock.

Scones: sieve flours, bicarbonate of soda, cream of tartar and salt. Rub in margarine until it resembles fine breadcrumbs. Add egg and milk and mix to a soft dough. Roll out to about 1.75 cm/¾" thick and cut out 12 small scones. Place scones on top of stew around the edge. Bake at No 8/230°C/450°F for 10-15 minutes or until golden brown.

Serves 6

270g CHO
2640 Calories } total

Beef & Nut Burgers

350 g/12 oz corned beef, mashed
1 large onion, finely chopped
50 g/2 oz peanuts, chopped
50 g/2 oz porridge oats
1 × 5 ml sp/1 tsp chopped parsley
4 × 15 ml sp/4 tblsp Worcester sauce
salt and pepper
1 egg, beaten

Coating:
beaten egg
wholemeal breadcrumbs

Thoroughly mix all ingredients and divide into 4, then shape into flat rounds. Dip in egg and coat in breadcrumbs. Place for 30-40 minutes in fridge. Fry in a little vegetable oil for 3-4 minutes each side until brown. Drain on absorbent kitchen paper and serve with a spicy sauce as part of a main meal or in a roll as a snack.

Serves 4

10g CHO
350 Calories } each

Beef & Vegetable Casserole

450 g/1 lb lean stewing steak
25 g/1 oz wholemeal flour
1 × 15 ml sp/1 tblsp salt
1 × 5 ml sp/1 tsp pepper
2 medium sized carrots, cut into batons
1 medium sized onion, sliced
25 g/1 oz low fat margarine
550 ml/1 pt beef stock
1 small can butter beans, drained
1 × 5 ml sp/1 tsp mixed spice
1 bayleaf

Trim excess fat off the meat and cut into 2.5 cm/1" cubes. Coat in seasoned flour. Seal in a hot pan. Add carrots, onions and beef stock and bring to boil, stirring continuously. Add butter beans, mixed spice and bayleaf. Cover and gently simmer for 1¾ — 2¼ hours or until the meat is tender.

Serves 4

60g CHO
1100 Calories } total

Beefburgers

450 g/1 lb minced beef
50 g/2 oz porridge oats
1 medium onion, finely chopped
1 × 5 ml sp/1 tsp mixed herbs
salt and pepper
4 wholemeal baps

Garnish:
1 tomato, sliced
4 slices onion
4 pieces lettuce
relish

Mix together mince, oats, onion and herbs and season well. Divide the mixture into four equal portions and form into balls, then flatten into a hamburger shape. Leave in the fridge for at least one hour. Grill under a medium hot grill for 15-20 minutes, turning once or until browned both sides.
Serve in the baps with a piece of lettuce, onion, tomato and spoonful of relish.

Serves 4

30g CHO
400 Calories } each

Bran Lamb Roll

1 medium breast of lamb, boned

Stuffing:

salt and pepper
1 onion, chopped
50 g/2 oz peanuts
50 g/2 oz Allbran cereal
50 g/2 oz wholemeal breadcrumbs
1 × 15 ml sp/1 tblsp chopped parsley
2 medium sized tomatoes, skinned
    and chopped
pinch of thyme
1 egg, beaten

Remove excess fat from lamb and season generously. Mix all dry ingredients together. Bind together with the beaten egg.
Spread stuffing over the lamb and roll up as for a swiss roll. Secure with string or cocktail sticks. Cook for 1½ hours at No 6/200°C/400°F and then for 30 minutes at No 4/180°C/350°F.

Serves 5

50g CHO
2100 Calories } total

40

Chilli Beef Cobbler

450 g/1 lb minced beef
1 large onion, chopped
1 × 2.5 ml sp/½ tsp chilli powder
275 ml/½ pt beef stock
400 g/14 oz can tomatoes
2 carrots, diced
salt and pepper
1 small can kidney beans, drained
1 small can butter beans, drained

Topping:
25 g/1 oz plain flour
1 × 15 ml sp/1 tblsp baking powder
150 g/5 oz wholemeal flour
pinch of salt
50 g/2 oz margarine
1 egg
a little skimmed milk

Cook onions and mince (without added fat) until browning. Pour off any excess fat. Add stock, tomatoes, chilli powder and diced carrots and season well. Cover and simmer for 35 minutes. Add kidney and butter beans and simmer for a further 15 minutes. Turn into an ovenproof casserole dish. Meanwhile sieve the dry ingredients and rub in fat until it resembles fine breadcrumbs. Add egg and enough milk to form a soft dough. Knead lightly, then roll out to 1.25 cm/ ½" thick. Cut out 10 scones and arrange on top of meat mixture. Cook at No 6/200°C/400°F for 25-30 minutes or until the scones are brown and crisp.
Serve with green vegetables.

Serves 5

175g CHO
2200 Calories } total

41

Continental Beef

1 × 10 ml sp/1 dssp low fat margarine
225 g/8 oz carrots, sliced
275 g/10 oz onions, chopped
450 g/1 lb lean braising steak, diced
425 g/15 oz can tomatoes
275 ml/½ pt beef stock
225 g/8 oz yellow split peas,
   soaked overnight
1 medium red pepper
1 medium green pepper
2 sticks celery, washed and sliced
225 g/8 oz bean sprouts
salt and pepper

Melt margarine in a large saucepan, add carrots, cover and cook on a medium heat for 2 minutes. Add onion and cook for a further 4 minutes. Turn up the heat, add braising steak, and stir every few minutes until all sides are browned. Drain off excess fat. Add tomatoes and stock, bring to the boil. Add split peas, cover and cook over a low heat for 1 ½ hours.

Core, de-seed and slice peppers, add to the simmering meat with the celery. Cook for a further 45 minutes or until meat and split peas are tender. Add bean sprouts and season to taste. Serve while bean sprouts are still slightly crunchy.

Serves 4-6

160g CHO
1900 Calories } total

Curried Lamb & Chapattis

450 g/1 lb cooked lamb, roughly chopped
1 × 15 ml sp/1 tblsp oil
1 onion, chopped
1 apple, peeled, cored and chopped
1 × 15 ml sp/1 tblsp curry powder
1 × 15 ml sp/1 tblsp wholemeal flour
275 ml/½ pt beef stock
2 × 15 ml sp/2 tblsp coconut
225 g/8 oz tomatoes, skinned and chopped
salt and pepper

Chapattis:
75 g/3 oz wholemeal flour
salt and pepper
3 × 15 ml sp/3 tblsp water

Quickly fry lamb in oil, drain and keep in warm place. Fry onion and apple until soft, stir in curry powder and flour and cook for 5 minutes. Add stock and coconut gradually to the curry mixture, stirring all the time. Add the lamb and tomatoes, season well and simmer for 25 minutes. Serve with chapattis.

Chapattis: mix seasoned flour with water, knead well and roll into 4 thin rounds. Grill for 2 minutes each side.

Serves 4

Curry
25g CHO
1320 Calories } total

Chapattis
10g CHO
60 Calories } each

*Illustrated

Meat Loaf

2 eggs, beaten
1 large onion, finely chopped
1 stick celery, finely chopped
1 × 15 ml sp/1 tblsp freshly chopped parsley
75 g/3 oz rolled oats
100 g/4 oz wholemeal breadcrumbs
350 g/12 oz minced beef
salt and pepper

Mix all the ingredients together, season well. Place in a loaf tin. Cover with foil and bake at No 4/180°C/350°F for 30 minutes. Drain off surface fat, re-cover and return to oven for a further 30 minutes.
Serve hot with jacket potatoes and vegetables or cold with salad.

80g CHO
1400 Calories } total

Mexican Beef

450 g/1 lb minced beef
3 beef stock cubes
425 ml/¾ pt boiling water
2 medium onions, chopped
50 g/2 oz lentils
4 × 15 ml sp/4 tblsp chilli sauce
1 × 10 ml sp/1 dssp Worcester sauce
4 × 15 ml sp/4 tblsp tomato purée
salt and pepper
50 g/2 oz green pepper, diced

Cook mince for 30 minutes in half the water with seasoning. Skim to remove any excess fat. Add the remaining water and beef stock cubes. Simmer for 30 minutes. Cook lentils for 20 minutes in boiling water, drain. Add to the meat mixture with chilli sauce, Worcester sauce, tomato purée and seasoning. Simmer for a further 5 minutes.
Just before serving add diced green pepper.

Serves 4

30g CHO
1000 Calories } total

Quick Chilli Con Carne

225 g/8 oz soya mince
225 g/8 oz minced beef
1 large onion, finely sliced
1 × 5 ml sp/1 tsp chilli powder
salt and pepper
425 g/15 oz can tomatoes
1 small can kidney beans, drained

Make up the soya mince as directed on the packet and add to the mince, then brown in a large frying pan, without any additional fat, for 5 minutes. Add onion, chilli powder and other seasonings, stir well. (If a hotter dish is required, add extra chilli powder). Add tomatoes, bring to the boil, then simmer gently, uncovered for 45 minutes. Add the kidney beans and cook for a further 5 minutes. Serve with boiled brown rice or bread.

Serves 4-6

*Illustrated

60g CHO
1280 Calories } total

Savoury Burgers

225 g/8 oz minced beef
25 g/1 oz rolled oats
25 g/1 oz cashew nuts, chopped
1 medium onion, chopped
1 carrot, finely chopped
1 stick celery, chopped
salt and pepper
1 egg, beaten

Mix all the ingredients together. Divide into four equal portions and form into round flat shapes on a floured surface. Rest for 10 minutes in fridge. Place in an ovenproof dish and bake covered at No 4/180°C/350°F for 20 minutes. Remove cover and continue cooking for a further 20-25 minutes until browned.
Serve with bread and salad or potatoes and green vegetables.

Serves 4

*Illustrated

5g CHO
165 Calories } **each**

Shepherd's Pie

450 g/1 lb minced beef
1 large onion, chopped
1 clove garlic, crushed
2 × 5 ml sp/2 tsp basil
25 g/1 oz wholemeal flour
150 ml/¼ pt beef stock
1 small can haricot beans, drained
salt and pepper
450 g/1 lb potatoes
75 g/3 oz cottage cheese
225 g/8 oz tomatoes, skinned and sliced
parsley

Peel, cook and mash potatoes. Leave to cool.
Cook mince over a very low heat in a large frying
pan until brown. Drain off fat. Add onion and
garlic and cook for 10 minutes. Stir in basil and
flour and gradually add stock. Add haricot beans
and season. Turn into an ovenproof dish. Beat
together the cold mashed potato and cottage
cheese, then pipe or spoon the mixture round the
edge of the dish. Arrange slices of tomatoes on
top and bake at No 6/200°C/400°F for 25-30
minutes or until golden brown.
Garnish with parsley and serve with green
vegetables.

Serves 4

160g CHO ⎫ total
1500 Calories ⎭

Stuffed Breast of Lamb

1 medium breast of lamb, boned
salt and pepper
2 medium onions, chopped
100 g/4 oz wholemeal breadcrumbs
1 × 15 ml sp/1 tblsp sage
2 egg yolks
1 small apple, cored and chopped
1 stick celery, chopped
50 g/2 oz walnuts, chopped

Remove all excess fat from the lamb and season well. Mix together onions, breadcrumbs, sage, egg yolk, apple, celery and walnuts. Spread the stuffing over the lamb then roll into a cylinder shape and tie round with string. Cook at No 4/180°C/350°F for 1¼ — 1½ hours or until the meat juices run clear when a skewer is inserted into the thickest part.

Serves 4

80g CHO
2200 Calories } total

Veal Casserole

25 g/1 oz low fat margarine
450 g/1 lb pie veal
2 large onions, sliced
1 × 5 ml sp/1 tsp paprika
1 × 15 ml sp/1 tblsp tomato purée
425 ml/¾ pt stock
salt and pepper
175 g/6 oz brown rice, washed
chopped parsley

Add veal to a hot dry pan. Turn until browning. Transfer to ovenproof dish. Add onions and margarine to pan and cook until transparent. Stir in paprika, tomato purée and stock and season well. Bring to boil and cook for 1 minute. Pour over veal then bake at No 3/160°C/325°F for 50 minutes. Add rice and cook for a further 55 minutes. Serve sprinkled with chopped parsley.

Serves 4

140g CHO
1600 Calories } total

Pork

Finding suitable pork recipes was difficult as pork is usually fatty and the leaner cuts are more expensive. In this section the emphasis has been on replacing traditional low fibre recipes with those which contain high fibre ingredients and accompaniments. You could experiment with your own favourite recipes using similar substitutes.

(left) Italian Pork

53

Bacon Roly-Poly

675 g/1½ lb cooked forehock of ham
    (lean meat only)
25 g/1 oz low fat margarine
1 onion, finely chopped
pinch of sage
1 × 15 ml sp/1 tblsp tomato purée
50 g/2 oz lentils
salt and pepper

Pastry:
225 g/8 oz wholemeal flour
1 × 5 ml sp/1 tsp baking powder
pinch of salt
100 g/4 oz shredded suet
150 ml/¼ pt water

Cook lentils in a little salted water until soft. Remove rind from bacon and cut meat from the bone, chop finely. Melt fat and cook onion until soft. Drain and add bacon, sage, tomato purée and cooked lentils. Season well.
Sift flour, baking powder and salt into a bowl, add suet and mix to a soft dough with water. Roll out to an oblong shape and spread with bacon mixture leaving about 2.5 cm/1" around the edge. Wet the edge of the pastry, roll up in a swiss roll shape. Wrap in greased greaseproof paper and then tin foil. Steam in a steamer for 2½ hours, or in a pressure cooker for 50 minutes.

Serves 6

180g CHO
3800 Calories } total

Italian Pork

25 g/1 oz low fat margarine
225 g/8 oz onions, peeled and chopped
450 g/1 lb minced pork
1 large clove garlic, crushed
1 × 10 ml sp/1 dssp mixed herbs
salt and pepper
150 ml/¼ pt dry white wine
2 × 15 ml sp/2 tblsp wholemeal flour
2 × 15 ml sp/2 tblsp tomato purée
½ chicken stock cube
350 g/12 oz button mushrooms, cleaned
   and sliced
225 g/8 oz wholemeal pasta shells

Melt margarine and gently cook the chopped onions until transparent. Add mince and cook for about 5 minutes until browned. Pour off any excess fat, add garlic, herbs, salt and pepper, and cook on a medium heat for 2 minutes. Turn up the heat, pour on wine and boil until the foam subsides. Mix in flour, tomato purée and crumbled stock cube. Cover and cook gently for 40 minutes, stirring often. Add the mushrooms and cook for a further 5 minutes. Meanwhile cook the pasta in plenty of boiling salted water for 10-15 minutes or until just tender. Drain, mix with the meat mixture and serve immediately.

Serves 4

*Illustrated

180g CHO
1800 Calories } **total**

Pork & Lentil Bake

100 g/4 oz lentils
100 g/4 oz bacon, de-rinded and chopped
100 g/4 oz onion, roughly chopped
100 g/4 oz mushrooms, roughly chopped
450 g/1 lb fillet of pork
1 egg, beaten
100 g/4 oz wholemeal breadcrumbs
3 × 15 ml sp/3 tblsp water

Bring lentils to the boil and simmer until like a purée. Fry bacon over a low heat without any extra fat, then remove from the pan and keep warm. Fry the onions and mushrooms until soft. Cut pork into strips about 2.5 cm × 7.5 cm/1" × 3" then dip first in the egg then breadcrumbs. Fry in the remaining bacon fat adding a little oil if needed. Layer the lentil purée, bacon mix and pork in an ovenproof dish. Add water, then cook at No 4/180°C/350°F for 45 minutes.
Serve with a green vegetable like runner beans and with plain mashed potatoes and gravy.

Serves 4

80g CHO
1700 Calories } **total**

56

Sausage & Lentil Loaf

50 g/2 oz lentils
1 medium onion, chopped
50 g/2 oz pigs liver
25 g/1 oz low fat margarine
1 egg
1 × 5 ml sp/1 tsp mixed herbs
225 g/8 oz pork sausagemeat
1 × 10 ml sp/1 dssp yeast extract
25 g/1 oz rolled porridge oats
1 × 10 ml/1 dssp tomato purée
salt and pepper

Wash lentils and boil in water for 15 minutes. Fry onion and liver in margarine for 10-15 minutes, until the onion is soft and the liver firm. Remove, drain and chop finely.

Thoroughly mix the onion and liver with the egg, herbs, lentils, sausagemeat, yeast extract, rolled oats and tomato purée. Season well.

Press mixture into a greased loaf tin and cover with tin foil. Place in a water bath and cook at No 3/160°C/325°F for 1¼ hours. Remove the tin foil and cook for a further 20 minutes.

This dish can be eaten hot or cold, and is especially nice with salads.

Serves 4

60g CHO
1200 Calories } total

Toad-in-the-Hole

100 g/4 oz wholemeal flour
2 eggs (size 3)
425 ml/¾ pt skimmed milk
450 g/1 lb pork sausages
2 rashers streaky bacon cut into 2.5 cm/1"
    pieces
1 medium onion, finely chopped
salt and pepper

Whisk flour, eggs, milk and seasoning together. Prick sausages well and place in a non-stick roasting dish. Add the bacon and onion. Cook in oven at No 5/190°C/375°F until sausages are browning. Drain off any fat. Increase oven temperature to No 6/200°C/400°F. Pour on batter and cook until golden brown and risen (approximately 30 minutes).
Serve immediately with gravy and vegetables of choice.

Serves 4

140g CHO
2000 Calories } **total**

Chicken

Chicken is a useful low fat main course ingredient but it needs to be made interesting for regular use. All the recipes in this section offer variety in flavour and texture and are guaranteed to please your friends and family.

(left) Chicken Kebabs, Chicken Paella

Chicken & Almonds

1 small onion, chopped
1 × 15 ml sp/1 tblsp oil
50 g/2 oz mushrooms, sliced
1 × 15 ml sp/1 tblsp cornflour
150 ml/¼ pt chicken stock
½ × 2.5 ml sp/¼ tsp ground ginger
½ × 2.5 ml sp/¼ tsp grated nutmeg
salt and pepper
1 egg (size 3)
150 g/5 fl oz natural yoghurt (small pot)
450 g/1 lb cooked chicken, skinned and
   cut into small pieces
25 g/1 oz toasted almonds

Heat oil and fry onion until brown, add mushrooms and fry for a further minute. Remove from heat and mix the cornflour into the onions and mushrooms. Gradually add chicken stock and bring to the boil stirring all the time. (If the sauce is too thick add a little more stock). Simmer for 5 minutes, then add the ginger and nutmeg. Season to taste. Beat egg and yoghurt lightly together and stir into sauce with chicken pieces. Heat gently, stirring continually, until the sauce begins to thicken. Sprinkle with toasted almonds and serve with brown rice.

Serves 3-5

30g CHO
1170 Calories } total

Chicken & Orange

4 chicken pieces
275 ml/½ pt water
1 onion, roughly chopped
1 carrot, grated
salt and pepper
juice of 2 oranges
½ green pepper, de-seeded and cut into
  thin strips
pinch of crushed cloves
pinch of allspice

Wash and clean chicken well, removing all surplus fat. Place chicken in water with onion and carrot and season well. Bring to boil and simmer for 40-50 minutes or until the chicken is tender. Lift out the chicken and place in a serving dish. Mix 150 ml/ ¼ pt of the cooking liquor with the orange juice. Season and add allspice and crushed cloves. Pour over chicken pieces and sprinkle on the strips of green pepper. Bake at No 6/200°C/400°F for approximately 30 minutes, basting frequently until chicken has browned. Serve with brown rice or jacket potatoes.

Serves 4

neg CHO
600 Calories } total

Chicken-Cider Casserole

Chicken and mushrooms cooked in a cider sauce.

25 g/1 oz onions, chopped
100 g/4 oz mushrooms, sliced
4 portions roasting chicken
50 g/2 oz wholemeal flour
50 g/2 oz low fat margarine
425 ml/¾ pt chicken stock
150 ml/¼ pt dry cider
salt and pepper

Fry onion and mushrooms in a little oil until soft, then place with the seasoned chicken portions in a casserole dish. Melt margarine, stir in flour and cook gently for 2 minutes. Remove pan from heat and very gradually add the stock and cider. Return to heat and bring to boil stirring all the time, then cook for a further 2 minutes. Pour over chicken and cook for approximately 1 hour at No 4/180°C/350°F. The chicken is cooked when the juice runs clear when knife is inserted in the thickest part.
Serve with brown rice or potatoes.

Serves 4

40g CHO
1160 Calories } total

Chicken Kebabs

Kebabs made with chicken, peppers, tomato, mushrooms and bacon.

1 × 5 ml sp/1 tsp saffron or turmeric
1 × 5 ml sp/1 tsp wholemeal flour
2 × 15 ml sp/2 tblsp vinegar
250 g/9 oz raw chicken, diced in
    2.5 cm/1" pieces
1 large tomato, cut into 8 pieces
8 small button mushrooms
4 rashers bacon
½ green pepper cut into 8 pieces
4 kebab skewers

Mix saffron or turmeric with flour and vinegar to make a thick paste. Toss chicken in the paste so that it is well covered. Cut each bacon rasher into two and roll up. Skewer chicken, bacon and vegetables alternately. Grill chicken until it is tender, turning during cooking.
Serve with brown rice.

Serves 2

*Illustrated

neg CHO
125 Calories } each

Chicken Paella

4 chicken joints, skinned
salt and pepper
1 × 15 ml sp/1 tblsp oil
2 onions, chopped
100 g/4 oz mushrooms, sliced
½ green pepper, de-seeded and chopped
4 tomatoes, skinned and chopped
2 sticks celery, chopped
225 g/8 oz can pineapple pieces
    in natural juice
275 ml/½ pt chicken stock
1 × 15 ml sp/1 tblsp soy sauce
pinch of garlic salt
175 g/6 oz brown rice, cooked

Season chicken joints and sauté in the oil for 20 minutes, then drain on kitchen paper. Add all the vegetables and pineapple pieces to the hot pan and fry for 2 minutes. Add pineapple juice, chicken stock, soy sauce, garlic salt and the chicken joints. Simmer for 30 minutes, add cooked rice then serve.
Could be garnished with parsley and lemon wedges.

Serves 4

180g CHO
1800 Calories } total

*Illustrated

Chicken Pilaff

550 ml/1 pt chicken stock
225 g/8 oz brown rice
1 × 2.5 ml sp/½ tsp salt
225 g/8 oz cooked chicken, cubed
1 onion, chopped
1 × 15 ml sp/1 tblsp parsley, chopped
1 small can kidney beans, drained
50 g/2 oz Edam cheese, grated

Cook rice in stock with salt for about 40 minutes or until just tender. Add chicken, onion, parsley and kidney beans to the drained rice and season to taste. Turn into a hot serving dish and sprinkle with grated cheese. Brown in a hot oven at No 6/200°C/ 400°F for about 10 minutes.

Serves 4

200g CHO
1360 Calories } total

Chilli Chicken

4 large chicken legs
1 × 10 ml sp/1 dssp low fat margarine
275 g/10 oz carrots, peeled and sliced
225 g/8 oz onions, peeled and chopped
425 g/15 oz can tomatoes
275 ml/½ pt chicken stock
1 × 5 ml sp/1 tsp chilli powder
225 g/8 oz lentils
1 large can kidney beans, drained
100 g/4 oz frozen runner beans
150 g/5 fl oz natural yoghurt (small pot)
salt and pepper

Skin chicken pieces. Melt margarine in a large saucepan, add sliced carrot, cover and cook on medium heat for 2 minutes. Add onions and cook until transparent. Fry chicken amongst the vegetables until golden brown, turning up the heat if necessary. Add the tomatoes, chicken stock, lentils and the chilli powder and simmer for 1 hour. Stir in runner and kidney beans and cook until beans are soft. Season to taste. Just before serving add the natural yoghurt and stir in well.

This can be a hot spicy dish, depending on how much chilli powder is added. It is a good idea to add it pinch-by-pinch until the desired taste is achieved.

Serves 4

220g CHO
2000 Calories } total

Chinese Chicken

450 g/1 lb boned, uncooked chicken
1 × 5 ml sp/1 tsp salt
2 × 15 ml sp/2 tblsp oil
1 × 15 ml sp/1 tblsp soy sauce
225 g/8 oz bean sprouts
2 sticks celery, chopped
50 g/2 oz button mushrooms
50 g/2 oz pineapple pieces in natural juice
½ small can kidney beans, drained
150 ml/¼ pt chicken stock
pepper
1 × 15 ml sp/1 tblsp cornflour
25 g/1 oz flaked almonds, toasted

Cut chicken into cubes, toss in salt and sauté for 3-5 minutes in oil. Add soy sauce, bean sprouts, celery, mushrooms, pineapple, kidney beans, pepper and stock and simmer for 15 minutes. Blend cornflour with a little water and stir into the chicken mixture. Bring slowly to boil, stirring all the time. Turn into serving dish and sprinkle with toasted almonds.
Serve with wholewheat pasta or brown rice.

Serves 4

40g CHO
1000 Calories } total

Slow-cook Chicken

4 chicken breasts
2 large carrots, chopped
1 onion, chopped
1 small aubergine, de-seeded and sliced
50 g/2 oz mushrooms, sliced
juice of ½ lemon
salt and pepper
275 ml/½ pt chicken stock

Bone and skin chicken breasts and chop into bite size pieces. Place in a dish with carrots, onion, aubergine and mushrooms. Pour in stock and lemon juice and season well. Bake at No 4/ 180°C/350°F for 1 — 1½ hours or until chicken is cooked.
Serve with either oven cooked brown rice or jacket potatoes.

Serves 4

20g CHO
480 Calories } total

Stuffed Chicken

1½ kg/3 lb chicken

Stuffing:
100 g/4 oz brown rice
2 onions, chopped
100 g/4 oz mushrooms, chopped
1 green pepper, de-seeded and chopped
1 × 15 ml sp/1 tblsp low fat margarine
50 g/2 oz mixed nuts, chopped
salt and pepper

Garnish:
25 g/1 oz mushrooms, sliced
25 g/1 oz toasted nuts
tomato wedges

Cook rice in boiling salted water until just tender. Fry onion, mushrooms and green pepper in the margarine, then mix with the cooked rice and remaining ingredients. Place stuffing in the chicken. Season well and bake at No 6/200°C/ 400°F for 1½ hours. Garnish with slices of lightly fried mushrooms, toasted nuts and tomato wedges.

Serves 4-6

80g CHO
1500 Calories } total

Liver & Kidney

This section has been included because liver and kidney are lower in fat than most other meats. Their flavour and texture are not always popular but they are inexpensive. There is little waste with them and they are quick and easy to prepare for evening meals.

Note: All offal meats are high in cholesterol and should not be eaten by people on low cholesterol diets.

(right) Liver & Chick-pea Pie

Italian Chicken Livers

Chicken livers served on a bed of wholewheat pasta.

2 medium onions, chopped
1 clove garlic, crushed
1 × 15 ml sp/1 tblsp oil
450 g/1 lb chicken livers, chopped
425 g/15 oz can tomatoes
1 × 15 ml sp/ 1 tblsp tomato purée
salt and pepper
275 g/10 oz wholewheat pasta

Sauté onions and garlic in oil. Add chicken livers and cook until brown. Drain off excess oil. Add tomatoes and purée. Bring to the boil, season well and simmer for 25 minutes. Meanwhile, cook pasta in boiling water until tender. Drain.
Serve liver on pasta.

Serves 4

160g CHO
1600 Calories } total

Liver & Bacon Risotto

225 g/8 oz brown rice
550 ml/1 pt chicken stock
225 g/8 oz pigs liver
100 g/4 oz back bacon
1 large onion, chopped
100 g/4 oz mushrooms, sliced
50 g/2 oz frozen peas
salt and pepper

Cook rice in stock for 20 minutes. Grill liver and bacon, then chop roughly and add to the rice with the onion and cook for a further 15 minutes (if a little dry add more stock). Add sliced mushrooms and peas and cook for a further 10 minutes. Season well then serve immediately.

Serves 4

180g CHO
1600 Calories } total

Liver & Chick-pea Pie

675 g/1½ lb potatoes
1 × 15 ml sp/1 tblsp butter and milk for
　　creaming potatoes
salt and pepper
1 small onion, finely chopped
25 g/1 oz low fat margarine
450 g/1 lb lambs liver, cut into bite-sized
　　pieces
2 × 15 ml sp/2 tblsp wholemeal flour
450 g/1 lb tomatoes, skinned and sliced
1 large can chick-peas, drained
1 × 15 ml sp/1 tblsp paprika
3 × 15 ml sp/3 tblsp natural yoghurt

Peel potatoes and cook in salted water for 15-20 minutes until tender. Mash with butter and enough milk to make a smooth thick purée. Season well and keep hot. Meanwhile in a large pan fry onion in margarine for 5 minutes. Coat liver pieces in the flour, add to the onions and brown quickly on all sides. Stir in tomatoes, chick-peas, paprika and seasoning. Cover and cook gently for 7 minutes. Meanwhile spoon or pipe potatoes around the edge of a warmed serving dish. Stir yoghurt into liver mixture and heat through. Pile in the centre of potatoes and serve immediately.

Serves 4-6

Illustrated

200g CHO
1920 Calories } total

Liver Stroganoff

225 g/8 oz calves or lambs liver
2 × 15 ml sp/2 tblsp wholemeal flour
salt and pepper
1 × 15 ml sp/1 tblsp oil
150 ml/¼ pt skimmed milk
150 g/5 fl oz yoghurt (small pot)
juice of half a lemon
1 × 15 ml sp/1 tblsp chopped parsley

Cut liver into small pieces. Toss in seasoned flour. Heat oil and fry liver gently until golden brown, drain. Stir in remaining flour and gradually add milk. Cook slowly, stirring all the time until the mixture thickens, then simmer for 5 minutes. Stir in the yoghurt and lemon juice. Spoon into serving dish and garnish with the chopped parsley.
Serve with brown rice or boiled potatoes and green vegetables.

Serves 4

40g CHO
680 Calories } total

Quick Liver Casserole

450 g/1 lb lambs liver, cut in
    2.5 cm/1" cubes
1 onion, chopped
175 g/6 oz carrots, chopped
100 g/4 oz frozen peas
400 g/14 oz can tomatoes
½ small can haricot beans, drained
425 ml/¾ pt vegetable stock
3 × 15 ml sp/3 tblsp tomato purée
salt and pepper

Place all ingredients in an ovenproof dish. Season well. Bake at No 4/180°C/350°F for 1¼ hours.

Serves 4

60g CHO
1140 Calories } total

Sweet & Sour Liver

225 g/8 oz wholemeal spaghetti rings
450 g/1 lb lambs liver cut into 2.5 cm/½" slices
2 × 15 ml sp/2 tblsp wholemeal flour,
salt and pepper
1 egg, beaten
2 × 15 ml sp/2 tblsp oil

Sauce:

1 small green pepper, de-seeded and sliced
1 small carrot, cut into batons
1 small onion, sliced
1 × 10 ml sp/1 dssp oil
275 ml/½ pt chicken stock
3 × 15 ml sp/3 tblsp white wine vinegar
1 × 10 ml sp/1 dssp clear honey
1 × 15 ml sp/1 tblsp cornflour
1 × 15 ml sp/1 tblsp soy sauce
salt and pepper

Sauce: fry onion, pepper and carrot, in oil until soft. Add stock, vinegar and honey then bring to the boil and simmer for 10 minutes. Blend in cornflour with a little cold water and soy sauce, add to the mixture and bring to boil, stirring all the time. Season to taste.

Cook spaghetti in boiling salted water until just tender (15-20 minutes). Coat liver in seasoned flour and egg. Fry in oil for 12-15 minutes. Serve liver on bed of spaghetti rings. Serve sauce separately or pour over liver and spaghetti.

Serves 4

200g CHO
2200 Calories } total

Turbigo Kidney

1 kidney
2 chippolata sausages
1 × 15 ml sp/1 tblsp oil
1 onion, chopped
50 g/2 oz mushrooms, chopped
1 × 10 ml sp/1 dssp wholemeal flour
1 × 5 ml sp/1 tsp tomato purée
2 bayleaves
150 ml/¼ pt water
salt and pepper

Halve kidney and remove the hard core, then fry with the sausages in oil for a minute or two until browned. Remove from pan. Fry onion and mushrooms until soft. Drain off excess fat. Stir in flour, tomato purée, bayleaves and water and heat until thickened. Replace kidney and sausages. Season well and simmer very gently for 15 minutes.

Serves 2

10g CHO
540 Calories } total

Fish

Fish can be tasty and interesting if flavourings and sauces are used. Remember when using tinned fish to choose those preserved in brine. If only tins of fish preserved in oil are available, drain the fish well before use.

(right) Cod with Mixed Vegetables

Cod in Yoghurt

4 cod steaks
salt and pepper
2 bayleaves
25 g/1 oz low fat margarine

Sauce:
450 g/20 fl oz natural yoghurt (large pot)
2 eggs
2 × 15 ml sp/2 tblsp capers
4 gherkins, chopped
rind of 1 lemon, grated
1 × 15 ml sp/1 tblsp parsley, chopped
salt and pepper
50 g/2 oz fresh wholemeal breadcrumbs

Place fish in small ovenproof dish. Season, add bayleaves and dot with margarine. Cover with foil and bake at No 5/190°C/375°F for 30 minutes. Drain the fish, remove skin and bones, then return to the cooking dish. Discard bayleaves. Beat together yoghurt, eggs, capers, gherkins, lemon rind, parsley and seasoning. Pour the sauce over and around the fish, sprinkle with breadcrumbs. Place dish in a water bath. Bake at No 4/180°C/350°F for 20 minutes or until the top is golden brown.
Garnish with parsley and serve with jacket potatoes and vegetables.

Serves 4

60g CHO
880 Calories } total

Cod with Mixed Vegetables

4 cod steaks
salt and pepper
1 × 2.5 ml sp/½ tsp dried parsley
2 large onions, finely chopped
4 sticks celery, finely chopped
25 g/1 oz low fat margarine
4 tomatoes, skinned and chopped
350 g/12 oz can sweetcorn

Place the steaks in an ovenproof dish with parsley and seasoning. Fry the onion and celery in the margarine until soft. Mix with the tomatoes, sweetcorn and a little more seasoning. Spoon over the cod steaks and bake at No 4/180°C/350°F for 40 minutes.
Serve with potatoes and green salad.

Serves 4

Illustrated

60g CHO
760 Calories } total

Fish Bake

Mackerel in a green bean and onion sauce with a crispy topping.

3 filleted mackerel
275 ml/½ pt skimmed milk
salt and pepper
1 × 10 ml sp/1 dssp chopped parsley
1 clove garlic, crushed
1 × 15 ml sp/1 tblsp vegetable oil
2 × 15 ml sp/2 tblsp wholemeal flour
150 g/5 oz onions, chopped
1 × 15 ml sp/1 tblsp low fat margarine
100 g/4 oz green beans
1 × 15 ml sp/1 tblsp wholemeal breadcrumbs

Season fish and poach in milk with parsley and garlic for 15-20 minutes. Drain, reserving the fish milk. Heat oil, add flour and cook for 3 minutes. Remove from heat, gradually stir in fish milk. Bring to the boil, stirring all the time and cook for a further 2-3 minutes. Fry onion in margarine until transparent. Add green beans and cook for approximately 10 minutes. Roughly flake the fish and add to sauce with onions and beans. Pour into a casserole dish, sprinkle with breadcrumbs and bake at No 6/200°C/400°F for 10 minutes or until browning.

Serves 4

40g CHO
1000 Calories } total

Fish Triangles

Pastry:
275 g/10 oz wholemeal flour
1 × 2.5 ml sp/½ tsp salt
150 g/5 oz margarine
cold water
milk to glaze

Filling:
450 g/1 lb can pilchards in tomato sauce
350 g/12 oz mushrooms, sliced
1 × 5 ml sp/1 tsp mixed herbs
salt and pepper

Mash pilchards and stir in mushrooms, herbs and seasoning.

Pastry: rub fat into flour and salt until mixture resembles fine breadcrumbs, adding just enough water to make a dough. Divide the pastry into 4 and roll each piece out to 15 cm/6" square. Divide the filling between each square. Brush edges with water or milk and draw one corner of each pastry square over to form a triangle, then seal firmly. Brush with milk and bake at No 5/190°C/375°F for 20-25 minutes or until pastry is crisp.
Can be served hot with vegetables or cold with a salad.

Serves 4

50g CHO
700 Calories } **each**

Smoky Bean Salad

450 g/1 lb smoked haddock
a little milk and water for poaching
1 large can butter beans, drained
4 tomatoes, skinned and quartered
1 lettuce, washed
1 hard boiled egg } garnish
nuts

Dressing: Mix together the following:
3 × 15 ml sp/3 tblsp natural yoghurt
2 × 15 ml sp/2 tblsp lemon juice
1 × 15 ml sp/1 tblsp chopped parsley
½ × 2.5 ml sp/¼ tsp curry powder
rind of 1 lemon, grated
salt and pepper

Poach fish in milk and water in a covered pan. Bring to the boil, remove from heat and leave to stand for 10 minutes. Drain thoroughly, remove skin and bones and flake. Add butter beans and tomatoes to fish. Bind fish mixture with the dressing and serve on bed of lettuce, garnished with slices of hard boiled egg and nuts.

Serves 4

60g CHO
800 Calories } total

Stuffed Herrings

4 herrings, gutted and boned
1 large apple, peeled and chopped
1 onion, grated
25 g/1 oz fresh wholemeal breadcrumbs
25 g/1 oz oatmeal
25 g/1 oz chopped parsley
salt and pepper

Topping:
25 g/1 oz low fat margarine
1 × 15 ml sp/1 tblsp wholemeal breadcrumbs
1 × 15 ml sp/1 tblsp oatmeal

Mix together the apple, onion, breadcrumbs, oatmeal, parsley and season well. Divide mixture into four and place in middle of each fish and roll up from head to tail, then pack into an ovenproof dish. For topping melt the margarine and pour over fish. Mix breadcrumbs and oatmeal and sprinkle over the top. Cook for 30 minutes at No 5/190°C/375°F or until fish is tender.

Serves 4

60g CHO
960 Calories } total

Tuna Bake

Ideal as a midday meal or snack.

25 g/1 oz low fat margarine
25 g/1 oz wholemeal flour
275 g/½ pt skimmed milk
100 g/4 oz cheddar cheese, grated
200 g/7 oz can tuna (in brine), drained and
    flaked
200 g/7 oz can sweetcorn
175 g/6 oz frozen peas
2 tomatoes, sliced
salt and pepper
1 small packet of cheese and onion crisps

Melt margarine and add flour and cook for two minutes stirring all the time. Remove from the heat and add the milk gradually. Bring to the boil, stirring all the time, then continue cooking for 2-3 minutes. Remove from heat. Add most of the grated cheese, tuna, sweetcorn, peas and season well. Place tomatoes at bottom of a lightly greased dish. Pour on the sauce. Crush crisps and sprinkle with remaining cheese over the top. Bake at No 3/160°C/325°F for 30-40 minutes.

Serves 4

80g CHO
1300 Calories } total

Pasta

In the past diabetics have tended to avoid pasta meals, but wholewheat pasta can be a tasty filling addition to the diet (see Food Values for CHO value). Don't be put off by the colour of uncooked wholewheat pasta — after cooking it lightens and the finished dish will look good at any table (look at the illustration for Canneloni & Red Beans opposite).
Wholewheat pasta is available from large supermarkets and health shops.

(right) Canneloni & Red Beans, Savoury Pasta

Canneloni & Red Beans

8 sheets (200 g/7 oz) wholewheat lasagne
1 large onion, finely chopped
25 g/1 oz low fat margarine
50 g/2 oz minced beef
425 g/15 oz can tomatoes
½ small can kidney beans, drained
1 × 2.5 ml sp/½ tsp mixed herbs
50 g/2 oz tomato purée
salt and pepper
150 ml/¼ pt water
50 g/2 oz branflakes, crushed
25 g/1 oz canned or frozen sweetcorn,
    cooked
parsley sprigs for garnish

Part cook lasagne in boiling salted water for 5-10 minutes. Drain and place on a clean work surface. Fry onion in margarine, add mince and fry until browned. Drain off excess fat. Stir in kidney beans, tomatoes, herbs, half the tomato purée and seasoning. Simmer for 10-15 minutes. Cut lasagne in half, place a little of the meat mixture on each. Roll up and secure with cocktail sticks if necessary. Place in an ovenproof dish. Mix remaining filling with the sweetcorn, half the branflakes and the rest of the tomato purée and water. Pour over filled tubes. Bake at No 4/ 180°C/350°F for 15 minutes.
Serve garnished with remaining branflakes and parsley.

Serves 4

*Illustrated

180g CHO
1110 Calories } total

95

Lentil Lasagne

25 g/1 oz low fat margarine
2 medium onions, chopped
50 g/2 oz bacon, chopped
450 g/1 lb minced beef
50 g/2 oz lentils
100 g/4 oz mushrooms, sliced
275 ml/½ pt beef stock
425 g/15 oz can tomatoes
50 g/2 oz tomato purée
1 × 5 ml sp/1 tsp mixed herbs
salt and pepper
1 garlic clove, crushed
225 g/8 oz wholewheat lasagne

Sauce:
50 g/2 oz low fat margarine
50 g/2 oz wholemeal flour
550 ml/1 pt skimmed milk
salt and pepper

Melt margarine, add onion, cook gently until soft. Add bacon and cook for two minutes. Stir in mince and garlic. Cook until mince has browned, stirring frequently. Pour off excess fat, add remaining ingredients. Cover and cook gently for 30 minutes. Season. Cook lasagne in boiling water for about 30 minutes or until the lasagne is just tender. Drain and rinse in cold water.

Sauce: melt margarine, stir in flour, return to the heat and cook for one minute, stirring continuously. Remove from heat and gradually stir in milk. Return to heat and bring to the boil, stirring all the time, then cook 2-3 minutes. Make layers of mince, lasagne and sauce ending with sauce, in an ovenproof dish. Sprinkle with a little Parmesan cheese and bake at No 6/200°C/400°F for 20 minutes or until heated through.

Serves 4

200g CHO
2400 Calories } total

Macaroni Bake

1 × 15 ml sp/1 tblsp oil
1 onion, chopped
450 g/1 lb minced beef
1 × 5 ml sp/1 tsp mixed herbs
225 g/8 oz can tomatoes
small can kidney beans, drained
salt and pepper
175 g/6 oz wholewheat macaroni
1 egg
100 g/4 oz cheese, grated

Fry onion in oil until soft. Add mince and fry until browned. Drain off excess fat. Stir in herbs, tomatoes, kidney beans, seasoning. Cover and simmer for 15 minutes. Cook macaroni in boiling salted water for 10-15 minutes or until just tender. Drain and rinse in cold water. Beat the egg and cheese together and stir in the macaroni. Place the meat mixture in an ovenproof dish and pile the macaroni mixture on top. Bake in oven at No 5/190°C/375°F for 30 minutes.

Serves 4

140g CHO
2200 Calories } total

Macaroni Mince Pie

150 g/5 oz short-cut wholewheat macaroni
100 g/4 oz soya mince *or*
225 g/8 oz minced beef
1 × 10 ml sp/1 dssp meat extract
425 g/15 oz can baked beans
1 × 5 ml sp/1 tsp cornflour
50 g/2 oz low fat margarine
25 g/1 oz wholemeal flour
275 ml/½ pt skimmed milk
salt and pepper
50 g/2 oz strong cheddar cheese, grated
1 tomato sliced for garnish

Cook macaroni in boiling salted water for 20 minutes or until just tender. Gently fry the mince then drain, or make up soya mince. Add meat extract, baked beans and cornflour.
Place margarine, flour and milk in a pan and bring to the boil, stirring all the time. Add the cooked, drained macaroni and season well.
Place the meat mixture in a large ovenproof dish. Spoon on the macaroni mixture, sprinkle with the grated cheese and garnish with the tomato. Place under a hot grill or bake at No 6/200°C/400°F until browned.
A mixture of soya and meat may be used to prepare an economical dish. If using only soya mince, more seasoning may be required.

Serves 4

200g CHO
1600 Calories } total

Pasta & Beans

6 slices lean bacon, chopped
1 medium sized onion, chopped
1-2 garlic cloves, crushed
2 sticks celery, chopped
275 ml/½ pt water
425 g/15 oz can tomatoes, chopped
1 × 15 ml sp/1 tblsp tomato purée
1 large can chick-peas, drained
3 × 15 ml sp/3 tblsp parsley, chopped
1 × 5 ml sp/1 tsp basil
salt and pepper
225 g/8 oz wholewheat pasta (macaroni,
    shells, etc)
1 × 15 ml sp/1 tblsp Parmesan cheese
2 hard boiled eggs

Dry fry bacon and drain on kitchen paper. Add onions, garlic and celery to pan. Sauté until soft. Add water, tomatoes, tomato purée, chick-peas, parsley, basil and season well. Add bacon. Simmer over a low heat for 5 minutes. Meanwhile cook pasta in boiling salted water until just tender, drain. Stir in the chick-pea mixture. Spoon into serving dish, sprinkle with Parmesan cheese and garnish with the sliced egg.

Serves 4-6

220g CHO
1660 Calories } total

99

Pasta with Cheese

225 g/8 oz wholewheat pasta
150 g/5 fl oz natural yoghurt (small pot)
100 g/4 oz cream cheese
2 × 15 ml sp/2 tblsp chopped chives
salt and pepper
extra chives for garnish

Cook pasta in boiling salted water for about 12 minutes or until just tender. Meanwhile, thoroughly mix yoghurt and cream cheese, cook over a gentle heat, stirring constantly until heated through. Stir in chopped chives and seasoning. Add the drained cooked pasta. Spoon into a serving dish, sprinkle with extra chives and serve hot.

Serves 4

160g CHO
1200 Calories } **total**

Savoury Pasta

1 large onion, chopped
1 large green pepper, de-seeded
    and chopped
25 g/1 oz low fat margarine
450 g/1 lb minced beef
425 g/15 oz can tomatoes
100 g/4 oz mushrooms, sliced
1 × 5 ml sp/1 tsp mixed herbs
25 g/1 oz tomato purée
seasoning
175 g/6 oz wholewheat pasta shells
salt and pepper
25 g/1 oz wheatflakes
25 g/1 oz cheese, grated
2 tomatoes, sliced

Fry onion and green pepper in margarine
until soft. Add mince and fry until brown, drain
off excess fat. Stir in canned tomatoes,
mushrooms, mixed herbs, tomato purée and
seasoning. Cover pan and simmer for 30 minutes.
Cook the pasta in boiling salted water for 15-20
minutes or until just tender. Drain and add to the
meat mixture. Place in a large ovenproof dish,
sprinkle with wheatflakes and cheese and arrange
tomatoes on top. Bake at No 4/180°C/350°F for
25 minutes or until the topping is brown. Garnish
with parsley and serve as a main course or as a
supper dish.

Serves 4

Illustrated

140g CHO
1800 Calories } total

Spaghetti Bolognese

1 onion, finely chopped
1 carrot, finely chopped
1 stick celery, chopped
1 clove garlic, crushed
1 × 15 ml sp/1 tblsp vegetable oil
100 g/4 oz minced beef
100 g/4 oz soya mince, reconstituted
225 g/8 oz can tomatoes
2 × 15 ml sp/2 tblsp tomato purée
1 bayleaf
150 ml/¼ pt beef stock
salt and pepper
275 g/10 oz wholewheat spaghetti
Parmesan cheese (optional)

Fry onion, carrot, celery and garlic in oil until soft. Add beef and soya mince and cook until lightly browned. Drain off excess fat. Stir in tomatoes, tomato purée, stock, bayleaf and season well. Simmer gently for 40 minutes. Meanwhile cook spaghetti in boiling salted water for 15 minutes or until just tender. Drain. Place in a serving dish, pour on the sauce and sprinkle with Parmesan cheese if liked.

Serves 4

200g CHO
1560 Calories } total

Spicy Chicken Pasta

A hot, filling main course.

1 large onion
1 large green pepper
100 g/4 oz mushrooms
250 g/9 oz boned chicken breast
25 g/1 oz low fat margarine
400 g/14 oz can tomatoes, drained and
    roughly chopped
1 × 15 ml sp/1 tblsp tomato purée
200 g/7 oz can apricots in natural juice
    drained and chopped
1 × 5 ml sp/1 tsp chilli powder
275 ml/½ pt water
salt and pepper
100 g/4 oz wholewheat spaghetti

Dice onion and pepper. Slice mushrooms and cut chicken into 2.5 cm/1" cubes. Melt margarine and fry onion and green pepper. Add chicken and mushrooms. When the chicken is browned, add tomatoes, tomato purée, apricots, chilli powder and water. Bring to the boil and simmer for 30-45 minutes or until chicken is tender. Break the spaghetti into 7.5 cm/3" long pieces and add to mixture. Continue to simmer, stirring frequently for a further 30 minutes or until spaghetti is cooked. Season to taste. (More water should be added if needed during final stages of cooking).

Serves 3

105g CHO
900 Calories } total

Rice

Brown (unrefined) rice is generally found to be more filling than white rice and its nuttier, fuller taste makes it an ideal accompaniment to many of the recipes used in this book. Rice can also be a quick and inexpensive main meal for the whole family. Brown rice is less likely than white rice to cause rapid rises in blood sugar after a meal. In white rice the outer layer of the grain which contains large quantities of B vitamins and dietary fibre is removed.

How to cook brown rice

Brown rice must not be cooked in the same way as white rice. You will find that it takes slightly longer to cook — but be careful not to overcook it. Properly cooked brown rice should have a slightly crunchy texture.

Here are two different methods of successfully cooking brown rice:

1. Pour the unwashed rice into salted boiling water and cook for approximately 45 minutes. Drain and rinse with boiling water before serving.
2. Wash the uncooked rice and pour into salted boiling water. Boil until tender (approximately 1 hour). Drain and serve.

(right) Nutty Pilaff

Chicken Jumble

825 ml/1½ pt chicken stock
225 g/8 oz brown rice
salt and pepper
25 g/1 oz low fat margarine
1 small onion, chopped
50 g/2 oz flaked almonds
100 g/4 oz mushrooms, sliced
25 g/1 oz tomato purée
1 small can kidney beans, drained
1 × 5 ml sp/1 tsp lemon juice
450 g/1 lb cooked chicken, roughly
    chopped *or*
cooked meat of choice
175 g/6 oz frozen beans

Bring stock to the boil, add rice, season well and simmer gently for 50 minutes. Add a little extra water if needed.
Meanwhile melt margarine, add onion and cook until soft. Add almonds and mushrooms and cook for 2 minutes. Stir in tomato purée, kidney beans, lemon juice and chicken (or other meat). Stir over low heat for a further 2 minutes.
Cook frozen beans in boiling salted water for 4 minutes, drain and add to chicken mixture.
When rice is cooked, drain and press into a lightly greased ring mould. Immediately turn out onto a large plate and spoon hot chicken mixture into the centre.

Serves 4

200g CHO
2000 Calories } **total**

Ham Risotto

175 g/6 oz brown rice
100 g/4 oz ham, chopped
50 g/2 oz cooked chicken, cubed
4 tomatoes, skinned and chopped
2 onions, chopped
2 carrots, diced
100 g/4 oz mushrooms, sliced
1 × 5 ml sp/1 tsp oil
825 ml/1½ pt stock
1 × 5 ml sp/1 tsp mixed herbs
salt and pepper
1 tomato for garnish

Cook rice in boiling salted water for 25 minutes or until just tender, then drain. Gently fry ham, chicken, tomatoes, onion, carrots and mushrooms in oil for 2 minutes. Add stock, herbs, season well and simmer for 30 minutes. When cooked, stir in the rice and serve garnished with slices of tomato.

Serves 4

140g CHO
1000 Calories } total

Nutty Pilaff

225 g/8 oz brown rice
1 large onion
1 × 15 ml sp/1 tblsp vegetable oil
1 chicken stock cube
700 ml/1¼ pt water
50 g/2 oz mushrooms
100 g/4 oz green or red pepper, sliced
salt and pepper
50 g/2 oz flaked almonds

Dice onion, fry with rice in oil for 5 minutes. Dissolve stock cube in water and add to rice. Slice mushrooms and pepper and stir into the rice mixture. Bring to the boil, season well. Reduce heat and simmer covered for 30 minutes. (If the liquid boils away, add a little more water). Add almonds and cook for a further 25 minutes or until the rice is cooked.
Serve hot with chicken pieces or liver.

Serves 4

*Illustrated

180g CHO } total
1200 Calories }

Oven Liver Risotto

450 g/1 lb lambs liver
2 onions, roughly chopped
1 red pepper, de-seeded and chopped
25 g/1 oz low fat margarine
825 ml/1½ pt brown stock
225 g/8 oz brown rice
50 g/2 oz frozen sweetcorn
50 g/2 oz frozen peas
50 g/2 oz frozen beans
1 × 5 ml sp/1 tsp mixed herbs
3 × 15 ml sp/3 tblsp tomato purée
4 shakes of Worcester sauce
1 beef stock cube
salt and pepper

Cut liver into small pieces and fry for 5 minutes in the margarine with onion and pepper, then place to one side. Pour stock in pan, add rice and simmer gently for 20 minutes until rice is just tender, then add the liver mixture and all remaining ingredients.
Place in a large ovenproof dish and bake at No 6/200°C/400°F for 25 minutes.

Serves 4

200g CHO
1800 Calories } **total**

Rice Stuffed Peppers

A starter or main meal when served with cold sliced meat.

175 g/6 oz brown rice
425 ml/¾ pt water
salt
4 green peppers
1 slice wholemeal bread
2 tomatoes, quartered
1 onion, roughly chopped
1 × 5 ml sp/1 tsp paprika
1 × 5 ml sp/1 tsp chilli powder
1 × 5 ml sp/1 tsp garlic salt
4 × 5 ml sp/4 tsp grated cheese

Cook rice in salted water. Meanwhile cut tops off peppers, de-seed, and gently cook in salted water for 5 minutes. Remove and drain. Tear bread into small pieces and mix well with tomato, onion, paprika, chilli and garlic salt. Blend a quarter of the mixture at a time in a liquidiser on a high speed for 15 seconds. Mix together the rice and all the blended mixture and fill peppers. Cover with foil and bake at No 4/180°C/ 350°F for 35 minutes. Place a teaspoon of grated cheese on top of each pepper and grill until bubbling. Serve immediately.

Serves 4

40g CHO
220 Calories
} each

Savoury Pilaff

50 g/2 oz low fat margarine
225 g/8 oz lambs liver, cubed
3 onions, finely chopped
50 g/2 oz pine nuts or chopped almonds
275 g/10 oz brown rice
1 × 2.5 ml sp/½ tsp mixed spice
salt and pepper
50 g/2 oz currants
1 large tomato, skinned and chopped
1 × 2.5 ml sp/½ tsp sage
1 × 2.5 ml sp/½ tsp parsley
825 ml/1½ pt meat stock

Gently fry liver in margarine until cooked. Drain and put aside. Fry onions until soft. Add nuts and rice and fry for 5 minutes stirring to prevent sticking. Add spices, seasoning, currants, tomato and herbs. Gradually pour in the stock, cover and cook over very low heat for approximately 30 minutes or until rice is tender and all water has been absorbed.
Stir in the liver. Cover and leave for 5 minutes before serving.

Serves 4

240g CHO ⎫
2000 Calories ⎬ total

Vegetable Mould

An easy rice and vegetable mould to serve with cold meat.

700 ml/1¼ pt chicken stock
225 g/8 oz brown rice
100 g/4 oz frozen mixed vegetables
salt and pepper

Bring stock to boil and add brown rice. Bring to boil again, then simmer gently for about 30 minutes or until all stock has been absorbed by the rice. Cook vegetables in salted water, drain and fold into the cooked rice. Season well. Firmly press into a round ring mould. Turn out when cold.

Serves 4

180g CHO
800 Calories } total

Meatless

This section is not just for vegetarians it is also for the many people who like the occasional meatless meal for taste and economic reasons. Nuts, peas, beans, soya products, eggs and cheese can be substituted for meat. The secret of preparing tasty meatless meals is to use herbs and flavourings.

(right) Cottage Cheese Quiche, Vegetable Curry

Cottage Cheese Quiche

Pastry:
175 g/6 oz wholemeal flour
1 × 2.5 ml sp/½ tsp baking powder
pinch of salt
75 g/3 oz margarine
2-3 × 15 ml sp/2-3 tblsp cold water

Filling:
2 large eggs
150 ml/¼ pt skimmed milk
100 g/4 oz cottage cheese
1 × 2.5 ml sp/½ tsp dry mustard
1 × 2.5 ml sp/½ tsp salt
large pinch of black pepper
1 large onion, finely chopped
2 tomatoes, sliced
2 × 5 ml sp/2 tsp Parmesan cheese

Rub fat into dry ingredients. Sprinkle cold water over mixture and mix to form a stiff dough. Roll out pastry and line a 20 cm/8" flan ring. Place a circle of greaseproof paper in the flan and fill with baking beans. Bake blind at No 6/200°C/400°F for 10 minutes. Remove paper and beans and return to oven for 5 minutes. Mix eggs and milk together, stir in cottage cheese, onion and all seasoning. Slice tomato and place in the bottom of pastry case. Pour in the filling and sprinkle with Parmesan cheese. Bake at No 6/200°C/400°F for 30-35 minutes or until brown, risen and set. Serve hot or cold.

Serves 4-6

Illustrated

120g CHO
1500 Calories } **total**

Egg & Nut Cutlets

1 onion, finely chopped
3 hard boiled eggs
50 g/2 oz wholemeal breadcrumbs
1 × 15 ml sp/1 tblsp fresh parsley, chopped
1 × 15 ml sp/1 tblsp wheatgerm
150 g/5 oz mixed nuts, chopped
salt and pepper
1 egg

Coating:
1 egg, beaten
50 g/2 oz wholemeal breadcrumbs
oil for frying

Fry onion in a lightly greased frying pan until just soft. Chop eggs and mix with breadcrumbs, parsley, wheatgerm, onion, nuts. Season well, bind with egg. Form into four cutlet shapes, dip in egg and coat with breadcrumbs. Rest for 10 minutes in fridge. Fry in a little oil until crisp and golden brown.

Serves 4

15g CHO
375 Calories } each

Mushroom Bran Burgers

2 large onions, chopped
2 garlic cloves, crushed
2 × 15 ml sp/2 tblsp vegetable oil
25 g/1 oz wholemeal flour
150 ml/¼ pt stock
1 × 5 ml sp/1 tsp yeast extract
225 g/8 oz mushrooms, sliced
75 g/3 oz Allbran
1 egg
50 g/2 oz wholemeal breadcrumbs
salt and pepper

Fry onions and garlic in oil until transparent. Stir in flour and cook for 2-3 minutes. Remove from the heat and gradually add stock, yeast extract and seasoning. Bring to the boil, then add the sliced mushrooms and Allbran. Mix together well and shape into 8 cakes. Coat the cakes in egg then breadcrumbs and fry in oil until golden brown.

Serves 4

10g CHO
100 Calories } each

Nutburgers

Serve instead of potatoes with any meat such as gammon or chops,
or serve as a snack with spicy tomato sauce and green salad.

50 g/2 oz Brazil nuts
50 g/2 oz cashew nuts
1 onion, finely chopped
1 large egg
25 g/1 oz wheatflakes, crushed
1 × 5 ml sp/1 tsp yeast extract
1 × 2.5 ml sp/½ tsp salt
1 × 15 ml sp/1 tblsp hot water
50 g/2 oz wholemeal breadcrumbs

Finely chop the nuts. Mix together with the remaining ingredients. Leave to stand for 10 minutes. Divide the mixture into eight and shape into flat round cakes. Rest for 10 minutes in fridge. Grill for 10 minutes on either side. Serve hot or cold.

Makes 8

5g CHO
110 Calories } each

Nut Croquettes

25 g/1 oz low fat margarine
25 g/1 oz wholemeal flour
150 ml/¼ pt skimmed milk
100 g/4 oz shelled peanuts
1 onion, finely chopped
1 carrot, finely chopped
1 × 5 ml sp/1 tsp yeast extract
2 sticks celery, finely chopped
salt and pepper
1 egg, beaten
50 g/2 oz wholemeal breadcrumbs
oil for deep frying

Melt the margarine, stir in flour and cook gently for 2-3 minutes. Remove from heat, gradually add milk. Bring to the boil stirring all the time. Cook for a further 2 minutes. Stir in nuts, onion, carrot, yeast extract and celery and season well. Form 6 flat cakes, dip in egg, coat with breadcrumbs. Rest for 10 minutes in fridge. Deep fry for a minute or until golden brown.

Serves 6

10g CHO
150 Calories } **each**

Nut Loaf

1 × 15 ml sp/1 tblsp wheatflakes, crushed
1 small onion
1 carrot
1 egg
150 ml/¼ pt skimmed milk
25 g/1 oz low fat margarine
salt and pepper
100 g/4 oz wholemeal breadcrumbs
50 g/2 oz walnuts, chopped

Grease a loaf tin and cover the inside with the crushed flakes. Roughly chop vegetables, place in a blender with egg, milk, margarine and seasoning. Liquidise until well mixed. Add breadcrumbs and nuts and turn into the prepared tin and smooth the top. Bake for approximately 1 hour at No 5/190°C/375°F until lightly brown and firm. Allow to stand for 10 minutes then turn onto a serving dish.
Serve cold with salad

60g CHO
780 Calories } total

Vegetable Curry

2 × 15 ml sp/2 tblsp vegetable oil
2 large onions, chopped
3 egg sized potatoes, diced
1 × 2.5 ml sp/½ tsp turmeric
3 × 15 ml sp/3 tblsp curry powder
2 × 10 ml sp/2 dssp wholemeal flour
275 ml/½ pt chicken stock
1 large carrot, diced
4 tomatoes, skinned and chopped
½ cauliflower, broken into florets
1 small can kidney beans, drained
1 small can butter beans, drained
100 g/4 oz frozen peas
salt and pepper

Heat oil and fry onions and potatoes for 5 minutes until soft. Add turmeric, curry powder and flour and cook the mixture for 5 minutes. Gradually stir in stock. Add carrot, tomato and cauliflower and season well. Cover and simmer gently for 30 minutes, then add kidney and butter beans. Cook for a further 20 minutes. If curry becomes dry, add a little more water. Stir in peas and cook for final 5 minutes.
Serve with brown rice, and usual curry accompaniments.

Serves 4

120g CHO
800 Calories } total

Pulses

Small amounts of pulses (dried beans, peas, etc) have been included in many of the recipes. These foods have consistently been shown to have beneficial effects on blood sugar control when they are included as part of the carbohydrate allowance at mealtimes. Their use also helps reduce the amount of meat used in meals which results in a reduced fat intake and savings on cost. Dried pulses are more economical and can replace canned pulses by substituting approximately one quarter of the quantity required ie instead of 1 large can use approximately 4 ounces of dried beans (weighed before soaking).

Using Pulses

All beans and peas (but not lentils) need to be soaked. During soaking they increase to about three times their size. Instead of soaking overnight the dried peas or beans can be brought to the boil and held at boiling point for at least two minutes then left to stand for two hours. They must then be drained and cooked (see table for cooking times).

All pulses must be brought rapidly to the boil and held at this point for at least 10 minutes before continuing. After cooking they will be ready for use in place of canned products.

(right) Lentil Pie

Guide to Cooking Times

Pulse	Minimum cooking time	Pressure cooking time
Aduki Beans (tiny, bright red bean)	1 hour	15 minutes
Black Beans (oval, shiny, black bean)	2½ hours	35 minutes
Black-eyed Beans/Peas (white bean with a small black "eye")	2 hours	20 minutes
Butter Beans (large, white kidney shaped bean)	1 hour	15 minutes
Chick Peas (yellow, "shrivelled" pea)	2 hours	45 minutes
Flageolets (pale green bean)	1 hour	15 minutes
Gungo Peas/Pigeon Peas (dull, brown pea)	2½ hours	35 minutes
Haricot Beans (small white bean)	2 hours	20 minutes
Kidney Beans (large, bright red bean)	1 hour	15 minutes
Lentils (tiny grey, green, yellow or orange seeds which are often split)	20 minutes	10 minutes
Lima Beans (small, green bean)	1 hour	15 minutes
Mung Beans (tiny, bright green beans)	30 minutes	10 minutes
Soya Beans (small beige bean)	3 hours	45 minutes
Split peas (yellow/green split pea)	40 minutes	10 minutes

Bean & Beef Curry

50 g/2 oz low fat margarine
1 medium onion, finely chopped
1 medium cooking apple, peeled
   and chopped
1 × 15 ml sp/1 tbsp wholemeal flour
2 × 15 ml sp/2 tblsp curry powder
425 g/15 oz can stewing or braising steak
275 ml/½ pt beef stock
1 large can kidney beans, drained
50 g/2 oz walnuts, chopped
25 g/1 oz desiccated coconut
1 × 15 ml sp/1 tblsp mango chutney
1 × 5 ml sp/1 tsp each jeerah
   (ground cumin), ginger, cinammon
salt and pepper

Fry onion and apple in margarine until soft. Stir in flour and curry powder. Cook for several minutes taking care not to burn. Gradually stir in meat, stock and kidney beans. Stir in chopped walnuts, coconut, mango chutney, ginger, jeerah and cinammon. Simmer for 30 minutes and season to taste.
Serve with brown rice.

Serves 4

80g CHO
1280 Calories } total

Bean & Liver Soufflé

275 ml/½ pt skimmed milk
1 bouquet garni
salt and pepper
25 g/1 oz wholemeal flour
25 g/1 oz low fat margarine
4 eggs, separated
100 g/4 oz lambs liver, cooked and
   finely chopped
1 small can kidney beans, drained and
   finely chopped

Bring milk and bouquet garni to the boil then leave covered to infuse for 30 minutes.
Melt margarine, stir in flour then cook for 2-3 minutes. Remove from the heat and gradually add the warm milk. Return to the heat and bring to the boil stirring constantly, then cook for 2-3 minutes. Remove from heat and gradually add the egg yolks followed by chopped liver and beans. Whisk egg whites until stiff, fold in and season to taste, then pour mixture into a greased soufflé dish. Bake at No 5/190°C/375°F for 25-30 minutes or until golden brown and well risen. Serve immediately.

Serves 4

60g CHO
900 Calories } total

Broad Bean Pie

900 g/2 lb shelled broad beans
1 large onion, chopped
1 × 2.5 ml sp/½ tsp dried sage
150 ml/¼ pt water
1 × 2.5 ml sp/½ tsp Marmite
3 × 15 ml sp/3 tblsp wholemeal flour
2 × 15 ml sp/2 tblsp skimmed milk
2 egg yolks, beaten
25 g/1 oz cheese, grated
50 g/2 oz fresh wholemeal breadcrumbs

Cook beans, onions and sage in water. When the beans are nearly cooked, drain. Mix the Marmite into the cooking liquor. Turn the vegetables into a greased ovenproof dish and pour over the gravy. Mix flour with milk until smooth, then stir in egg yolks and cheese. Spread this mixture over the vegetables, sprinkle with breadcrumbs and bake at No 4/180°C/350°F for 30 minutes or until golden brown.

Serves 6

220g CHO
1450 Calories } total

Chicken Cassoulet

450 g/1 lb haricot beans, soaked
1 leek, finely chopped
4 onions, chopped
225 g/8 oz streaky bacon, roughly chopped
1650 ml/3 pt chicken stock
6 chicken drumsticks, skinned
1 × 2.5 ml sp/½ tsp garlic salt
1 × 5 ml sp/1 tsp black pepper
1 × 5 ml sp/1 tsp thyme
1 bouquet garni
350 g/12 oz tomatoes, skinned and chopped
100 g/4 oz garlic sausage, sliced
3 sticks celery, chopped
150 ml/¼ pt dry white wine

Place drained beans, leek, onion, bacon, stock, drumsticks and seasoning in a large pan and bring to the boil. Hold at boiling point for 10-15 minutes. Simmer for 1¼ hours. Add remaining ingredients and turn into an ovenproof dish and bake for a further 1 — 1¼ hours at No 7/220°C/425°F.

Serves 6

220g CHO
3000 Calories } total

Curried Lentil Bobatie

100 g/4 oz lentils
425 ml/¾ pt water
1 × 15 ml sp/1 tblsp curry powder
1 × 2.5 ml sp/½ tsp salt
3 onions, thinly sliced
1 × 15 ml sp/1 tblsp vegetable oil
225 g/8 oz minced beef
3 tomatoes, thinly sliced
1 egg
150 g/5 fl oz yoghurt (small pot)
25 g/1 oz wholemeal flour

Cook lentils in water with curry powder and salt until tender and like a thick purée.
Cook onions in oil until transparent. Add mince and fry until brown. Drain off excess fat. Add tomatoes and cook for a further 5 minutes. Stir meat mixture into the lentil mixture and turn into an ovenproof dish. Blend the egg, yoghurt and flour together and pour over top of the mixture. Bake at No 4/180°C/350°F for 30 minutes.

Serves 4

80g CHO
1000 Calories } total

Lentil Loaf

225 g/8 oz lentils
825 ml/1½ pt water
1 × 15 ml sp/1 tblsp yeast extract
2 small onions, chopped
1 small green pepper de-seeded
   and chopped
1 clove garlic, crushed
25 g/1 oz low fat margarine
2 tomatoes, chopped
2 sticks celery, chopped
1 small apple, cored and chopped
75 g/3 oz wholemeal breadcrumbs
1 × 2.5 ml sp/½ tsp marjoram
1 × 2.5 ml sp/½ tsp sage
1 × 5 ml sp/1 tsp parsley, chopped
50 g/2 oz walnuts, chopped
2 eggs, beaten
salt and pepper
pinch of nutmeg

Simmer lentils in water until tender and all liquid has been absorbed. Add yeast extract. Fry onion, pepper and garlic in margarine until soft. Drain. Add to lentils with remaining ingredients and season to taste. Press mixture into a greased round 20 cm/8" cake tin and bake at No 4/180°C/350°F for 50 minutes until brown and firm to touch. Cool for 10 minutes before turning out onto a serving dish. Serve cold with a salad or hot with tomato sauce.

Serves 4

160g CHO
1400 Calories } total

Lentil Pie

100 g/4 oz lentils
100 g/4 oz peeled potato, sliced
1 large onion, roughly chopped
1 large carrot, roughly chopped
825 ml/1½ pt stock
1 × 15 ml sp/1 tblsp Worcester sauce
1 × 2.5 ml sp/½ tsp mixed herbs
salt and pepper
100 g/4 oz wholewheat macaroni
50 g/2 oz Edam cheese, grated
3 slices red pepper for garnish

Liquidise the raw lentils. Boil potato, onion and carrot in salted water for 15 minutes, drain. Add to lentils, with stock, Worcester sauce, mixed herbs and seasoning. Simmer in a covered pan for one hour. Liquidise or purée this mixture. Meanwhile cook macaroni in boiling, salted water until just tender, drain and add to the lentil mixture.

Turn into an ovenproof dish, sprinkle with cheese and brown under a hot grill. Serve garnished with red pepper and parsley.

Serves 4-6

**140g CHO
900 Calories** } total

Red Bean Loaf

1 small can kidney beans, drained
1 × 5 ml sp/1 tsp yeast extract
1 garlic clove, crushed
2 tomatoes, skinned and chopped
2 onions, chopped
1 dessert apple, cored and chopped
50 g/2 oz wholemeal breadcrumbs
25 g/1 oz Weetabix or wheatflakes, crushed
1 green pepper, de-seeded and chopped
1 × 2.5 ml sp/½ tsp marjoram
1 × 2.5 ml sp/½ tsp sage
2 × 5 ml sp/2 tsp parsley, chopped
pinch of grated nutmeg
2 eggs, beaten

Thoroughly mix all ingredients and place in a greased loaf tin. Bake at No 4/180°C/350°F for one hour. Rest for 10 minutes in tin before turning out.
Serve hot or cold.

80g CHO
600 Calories } total

Soya Loaf

100 g/4 oz soya beans, soaked
275 ml/½ pt tomato juice
450 g/1 lb lambs liver, finely minced
3 × 10 ml sp/3 dssp capers, chopped
100 g/4 oz green pepper, finely chopped
100 g/4 oz onion, finely chopped
1 × 10 ml sp/1 dssp anchovy essence
1 clove garlic, crushed
1 egg, beaten

Cook soya beans in boiling water for about 45 minutes or until tender, then liquidise with tomato juice. Combine liver with capers, onion, green pepper, anchovy essence, garlic, soya bean mixture and egg. Press into a lightly greased loaf tin. Cook uncovered at No 4/180°C/350°F for 1 hour.

Serve loaf hot with gravy or a tomato sauce as it can be slightly dry. Use carrots, sweetcorn or peas as accompaniments to give added colour.

30g CHO
1300 Calories } total

Stuffed Potatoes

4 large potatoes
(each approximately 150 g/5 oz)

Filling:
1 large can kidney beans, drained
1 large onion, chopped
200 g/7 oz can tomatoes
2 × 15 ml sp/2 tblsp tomato purée
1 × 15 ml sp/1 tblsp paprika
salt and pepper

Scrub and wash potatoes thoroughly, prick with a fork then bake at No 4/180°C/350°F for 1 hour or until soft.
Meanwhile fry onion in a drop of oil, until nearly transparent. Stir in tomatoes, kidney beans, tomato purée, paprika and season well. Cook over a low heat for 20 minutes. Halve potatoes, scoop out the insides and mix with filling. Pile back into the skins and serve immediately.

Serves 4

45g CHO
220 Calories } each

Vegetables

Vegetables give colour, flavour and bulk to meals, but when they are just boiled they can be uninteresting.
In this section are a few ideas for using vegetables as more interesting accompaniments to main meals or as meals themselves.

(right) Vegetable Moussaka

Cauliflower Bake

1 large cauliflower
4 tomatoes, skinned and halved
225 g/8 oz mushrooms

Sauce:
25 g/1 oz low fat margarine
25 g/1 oz wholemeal flour
275 ml/½ pt skimmed milk
225 g/8 oz cottage cheese, sieved
salt and pepper

Topping (optional):
25 g/1 oz dry roasted peanuts, chopped

Break cauliflower into large florets. Cook in salted boiling water until just tender.
Place tomatoes in an ovenproof dish. Halve mushrooms, toss quickly in a hot, dry pan. Place with tomatoes in a warm oven to gently heat through.
Melt margarine, stir in flour, cook for a few minutes. Remove from heat, gradually stir in milk. Return to heat and stir continuously until thickened. Cook for 2-3 minutes. Add cottage cheese and season well. Turn cauliflower into serving dish, surround with tomatoes and mushrooms. Pour over sauce. Garnish with peanuts if liked.

Serves 4

40g CHO
640 Calories } **total**

Cauliflower & Walnuts

Serve as a vegetable or lunchtime snack.

1 medium cauliflower
1 slice wholemeal bread lightly spread
**   with low fat margarine.**
25 g/1 oz low fat margarine
25 g/1 oz walnuts
275 ml/½ pt skimmed milk
25 g/1 oz wholemeal flour
salt and pepper

Boil cauliflower in salted water until just tender. Drain and place in an ovenproof dish. Cut bread into small pieces and place in a blender with the walnuts. Blend until the bread is in crumbs and the nuts finely chopped. Place milk, flour, margarine, salt and pepper in a pan and bring to the boil stirring all the time. (Add more milk if the sauce is too thick). Cook gently for 2-3 minutes. Pour the sauce over the cauliflower, sprinkle with the crumb mixture, then brown under a grill.

Serves 4

40g CHO
500 Calories } total

Chicken Stuffed Onions

2 chicken joints, skinned
4 large French onions
100 g/4 oz mushrooms, chopped
100 g/4 oz wholemeal breadcrumbs
2 sticks celery, chopped
50 g/2 oz frozen or canned sweetcorn
1 × 5 ml sp/1 tsp paprika
salt and black pepper

Poach chicken joints in a little well seasoned water until tender. Remove the meat from the bone and roughly chop. Poach onions in a little water for 20-25 minutes or until tender.
Mix together mushrooms, breadcrumbs, chicken, celery, sweetcorn, paprika and season well. Remove the centres from the onions and chop, then add to the remaining ingredients. Pile the filling into the onion cases and bake for 15 minutes at No 4/180°C/350°F.

Serves 4

25g CHO
175 Calories } **each**

Ratatouille

2 × 15 ml sp/2 tblsp olive oil
450 g/1 lb aubergines, cored
450 g/1 lb courgettes
400 g/14 oz can tomatoes
1 green pepper, de-seeded
1 red pepper, de-seeded
1 medium onion
1 clove garlic, crushed
salt and pepper

Heat oil in a heavy pan. Chop all the vegetables
into bite-sized pieces and place in the oil. Add
crushed garlic and seasoning. Mix well. Heat until
the mixture is bubbling, then reduce the heat and
cook covered for 1 — 1½ hours or until the
vegetables are tender and have intermingled with
each other.

Serves 4

40g CHO
520 Calories } total

Savoury Baked Potatoes

*Three different fillings for baked potatoes which make a change from
a knob of butter or grated cheese.
The quantities given are for 2 (175 g/6 oz) potatoes.*

1st Filling:

2 slices cooked ham, chopped
¼ cucumber, diced
150 g/5 fl oz natural yoghurt (small pot)

2nd Filling:

100 g/4 oz cottage cheese with chives

3rd Filling:

2 large tomatoes, skinned and chopped
1 medium onion, finely chopped
50 g/2 oz Edam cheese, diced
salt and pepper

Wash and scrub potatoes, cut a cross on one side of each potato. Bake at No 4/180°C/350°F for approximately 1 — 1½ hours or until tender. When potatoes are cooked, cut in half and carefully scoop out the potato with a teaspoon, leaving the skin as clean as possible. Mash the potato and mix with the ingredients of the chosen filling. Fill potato skins with the mixture and return to oven for approximately 15 minutes or until warmed through.

30g CHO
175-200 Calories } **each**

Stuffed Aubergines

225 g/8 oz boned chicken breast
1 × 15 ml sp/1 tblsp soy sauce
2 aubergines
salt
175 g/6 oz mushrooms
1 small red pepper
1 rasher bacon

Marinate chicken in soy sauce for 30 minutes. Cut aubergines in half lengthways and remove seed and pulp. Reserve a little to mix with other ingredients. Sprinkle with salt and leave upside down for 30 minutes. Meanwhile chop mushrooms, red pepper and bacon. Gently fry bacon, add mushrooms, aubergine and pepper and fry until soft. Chop chicken and mix with the vegetables. Rinse and dry aubergines and fill with the chicken stuffing. Cover and bake at No 4/ 180°C/350F for 45 minutes.
Serve with rice or potatoes.

Serves 4

neg CHO
100 Calories } each

146

Stuffed Onions

4 medium onions, peeled
25 g/1 oz wholemeal breadcrumbs
salt and pepper
25 g/1 oz cottage cheese
1 × 15 ml sp/1 tblsp low fat margarine

Sauce:
25 g/1 oz low fat margarine
25 g/1 oz wholemeal flour
150 ml/¼ pt skimmed milk
50 g/2 oz cottage cheese, sieved
150 ml/¼ pt onion liquid
salt and pepper

Cook onions in boiling salted water for 15-20 minutes, drain. Reserve the onion liquid for the sauce. Scoop out onion centres using small spoon and a pointed knife and chop finely. Mix onion, breadcrumbs, seasoning and cottage cheese together, moistening with a little milk if necessary. Fill onion shells, transfer to a greased ovenproof dish, dot with knobs of margarine. Bake at No 6/200°C/400°F for 20-30 minutes or until browned.
Sauce: melt margarine and stir in flour, cook gently for 2-3 minutes. Remove from heat, gradually add liquids. Bring to the boil, stirring all the time, then cook for further 2 minutes. Stir in cottage cheese, season to taste and pour over the onions and serve.

Serves 4

10g CHO
130 Calories } each

Stuffed Peppers (1)

4 large peppers
100 g/4 oz brown rice, cooked
75 g/3 oz cooked ham, chopped
50 g/2 oz peas
1 onion, chopped
salt and pepper
1 × 10 ml sp/1 dssp tomato purée
25 g/1 oz cheese, grated
25 g/1 oz wholemeal breadcrumbs

Remove tops of peppers, core and de-seed. Blanch in boiling water for 5 minutes.
Mix together the cooked rice, ham, peas and onion and season well. Moisten if necessary with a little tomato purée. Divide this mixture between the four peppers. Sprinkle with the grated cheese and breadcrumbs. Place in an ovenproof dish and bake at No 5/190°C/375°F for 20 minutes or until the peppers are soft and the cheese melted.
Serve with a salad or as a starter.

Serves 4

25g CHO
215 Calories } each

Stuffed Peppers (2)

2 medium green peppers
50 g/2 oz mushrooms, chopped
175 g/6 oz cottage cheese
1 egg
2 sticks celery, chopped
1 Weetabix, crushed
1 × 5 ml sp/1 tsp mixed herbs

Slice tops off peppers and de-seed (keep tops). Place in boiling salted water for 10 minutes. Mix all the remaining ingredients and spoon into the drained peppers. Replace their lids, put in a greased dish, cover with foil and bake at No 5/ 190°C/375°F for 20 minutes.

Serves 2

10g CHO
200 Calories } each

Vegetable Chop Suey

1 × 15 ml sp/1 tblsp oil for frying
225 g/8 oz celery, chopped
1 large onion, chopped
100 g/4 oz green pepper, de-seeded and sliced
225 g/8 oz cabbage, chopped
100 g/4 oz red cabbage, chopped
150 ml/¼ pt stock
2 × 15 ml sp/2 tblsp soy sauce
salt and pepper
1 small can kidney beans, drained
100 g/4 oz mushrooms, sliced
175 g/6 oz bean sprouts

Heat oil then add all the vegetables except the kidney beans, mushrooms and bean sprouts. Keep turning the vegetables so they gently cook without browning (about 5-10 minutes). Add the stock, soy sauce and season well. Bring to the boil and simmer until the vegetables are almost tender. Stir in kidney beans, mushrooms and bean sprouts, and warm them through. When cooked the vegetables should be just tender and very little cooking liquid should be left.
Serve immediately.

Serves 4

40g CHO
460 Calories } total

Vegetable Moussaka

2 medium onions, sliced
2 sticks celery, chopped
1 small parsnip
3 medium carrots, sliced
25 g/1 oz low fat margarine
3 × 15 ml sp/3 tblsp wholemeal flour
400 g/14 oz can tomatoes in tomato juice
1 large can kidney beans, drained
salt and pepper

Sauce:
50 g/2 oz low fat margarine
50 g/2 oz wholemeal flour
425 ml/¾ pt skimmed milk
salt and pepper
2 eggs, beaten
50 g/2 oz mature chedder, grated
tomato slices for garnish

Slowly cook onions, celery, parsnip and carrots in margarine, in a covered pan. When the parsnip is soft, blend the flour with a little of the tomato juice and stir into the sautéd vegetables. Add the tomatoes, remaining juice and kidney beans, season well. Cook over a medium heat until the mixture thickens, stirring continuously. Turn into a large ovenproof dish.
Sauce: melt margarine, add flour and milk bring to the boil, stirring continuously. Season and cook for a further 2 minutes. Remove from heat, slowly add the beaten egg. Mix and pour over the vegetables. Sprinkle with cheese. Bake at No 6/200°C/400°F for 40 minutes, until brown and set.

Serves 4-6

*Illustrated

160g CHO
1400 Calories } total

151

Salads

A salad doesn't mean a lettuce leaf with a meal. A salad can be made with a variety of fresh vegetables, fruits and cold cooked items mixed together to form either an accompaniment to a rich meal or as a meal in itself. For instance a portion of pizza or quiche and a portion of salad could be served together, or a portion of Corn and Tuna Salad served with wholemeal bread would make an ideal midday meal in itself. The secret of a good salad is to use only fresh ingredients.

If a binding agent is needed a little vinegar or natural yoghurt should do the trick.

(right) Fruit Coleslaw, Bean & Rice Salad, Corn & Tuna Salad, Red Bean Salad (right, back), White Cabbage Salad, Salad Surprise (front).

Bean & Rice Salad

1 large can kidney beans, drained
2 tomatoes, sliced
50 g/2 oz brown rice
1 onion, chopped
150 g/5 fl oz natural yoghurt (small pot)
lemon juice to taste

Cook rice in boiling salted water for 40 minutes or until just tender. When rice is cold, mix together with all other ingredients, adding lemon juice to taste.

*Illustrated

120g CHO
600 Calories } **total**

Corn & Tuna Salad

350 g/12 oz can sweetcorn, drained
200 g/7 oz can tuna (in brine), drained
    and mashed.
1 hard boiled egg, chopped
1 carrot, grated
2 sticks celery, chopped
vinegar to taste

Mix together all ingredients, adding vinegar to taste.

Illustrated

60g CHO
560 Calories } total

Fruit Coleslaw

A coleslaw using dried fruit and apple with a yoghurt dressing.

450 g/1 lb white cabbage
2 medium carrots
25 g/1 oz sultanas
25 g/1 oz raisins
2 small onions
1 medium crisp apple
150 g/5 fl oz natural yoghurt (small pot)

Finely shred white cabbage and grate carrot. Soak sultanas and raisins in boiling water for about 10 minutes, drain. Finely chop onion and apple. Mix ingredients together thoroughly with natural yoghurt. Serve on its own or accompanying other dishes.

Illustrated

80g CHO
380 Calories } **total**

Red Bean Salad

450 g/1 lb apples, peeled, cored, cubed
    and soaked in a little lemon juice
50 g/2 oz walnuts, roughly chopped
3 sticks celery, chopped
½ small can kidney beans, drained
50 g/2 oz cooked brown rice
25 g/1 oz sultanas

Dressing:
75 g/3 oz orange yoghurt (½ small pot) ⎫
few drops tabasco   ⎬ mixed
salt and pepper   ⎭
sliced orange for decoration

Mix together all the salad ingredients, toss in the yoghurt dressing and decorate with slices of orange.

120g CHO ⎫
800 Calories ⎬ total

*Illustrated

Salad Surprise

4 red apples, cored
little lemon juice
150 ml/¼ pt water
50 g/2 oz walnuts, roughly chopped
50 g/2 oz shelled peanuts
1 head celery, chopped
450 g/20 fl oz natural yoghurt (large pot)

Dice 2 of the apples, slice remaining 2 and place in water and lemon juice to stop them browning. Drain the diced apples and mix with nuts, celery and natural yoghurt. Place in a large serving dish with the sliced apples around the edge.

*Illustrated

80g CHO
800 Calories } total

Turkey Rice Salad

A brown rice salad using mushrooms and cooked turkey.
Other cooked meats could be used instead of turkey.

100 g/4 oz brown rice
275 ml/½ pt chicken stock
275 ml/½ pt skimmed milk
225 g/8 oz mushrooms, sliced
1 × 5 ml sp/1 tsp lemon juice
100 g/4 oz cooked turkey
1 × 5 ml sp/1 tsp parsley
salt and pepper

Cook rice in stock and milk until all the liquid is absorbed. Cook the mushrooms for 3 minutes in a little boiling water with the lemon juice. Chop turkey. Add with mushrooms to the rice. Stir in parsley and season to taste.

80g CHO
550 Calories } total

White Cabbage Salad

¼ white cabbage, finely sliced
1 red apple, cored and sliced
small packet dry roasted peanuts
1 Shredded Wheat
1 orange, skinned, de-pithed and segmented
2 sticks celery, chopped

Dressing:
2 × 15 ml sp/2 tblsp mayonnaise
2 × 15 ml sp/2 tblsp skimmed milk } mixed

Pull Shredded Wheat apart so it is in long strands. Mix together with all the ingredients, then toss in the dressing.

Illustrated

40g CHO
460 Calories } total

Yoghurt Crunch

300 g/10 fl oz natural yoghurt (2 small pots)
2 sticks celery
½ cucumber
½ green pepper, de-seeded
½ red pepper, de-seeded
salt and black pepper
50 g/2 oz walnuts, finely chopped

Finely chop all vegetables, mix with yoghurt and season well. Serve in individual bowls, sprinkled with finely chopped walnuts.
This can be served with triangles of toast or as an accompaniment to the main course.

20g CHO
440 Calories } total

Puddings

There are few things better than fruit to end a meal for a diabetic but occasionally more variety is wanted. It is possible to make a suitable alternative by concentrating on the quality of the carbohydrate ingredients used and by reducing the fat and calorie content of a pudding by using skimmed milk and low fat margarines wherever possible.

Fructose (fruit sugar) has been used in these recipes as a bulk sweetener because of the possible side effects of sorbitol.

However, if your doctor or dietitian prefers you to use sorbitol, do so, but you will probably find you will have to use more and therefore increase the calorie content of the pudding. (25 g/1 oz sorbitol contains approximately 110 calories). Remember that no more than 50 grams of fructose should be consumed in any one day.

(left) Apple Nut Crisp

Apple Envelopes

Pastry:
225 g/8 oz wholemeal flour
100 g/4 oz margarine
water to mix

Filling:
2 large cooking apples
1 × 5 ml sp/1 tsp mixed spice
50 g/2 oz nuts, chopped
liquid sweetener to taste

Make pastry. Peel, core and slice apples, simmer gently in a little water until soft but still retaining shape. Add sweetener, mixed spice and nuts. Divide pastry in 4 and roll each piece of pastry to a square approximately 7.5 cm/3" square. Place the apple mixture in centre of each square, dampen the edges of pastry and draw together to form an envelope shape, sealing firmly. Bake at No 7/220°C/425°F for 25 minutes or until pastry is crisp.

Serves 4

45g CHO
450 Calories } **each**

Apple Nut Crisp

An apple and custard pudding with a crispy nut topping.

350 g/12 oz cooking apples
1 × 10 ml sp/1 dssp fructose
1 × 15 ml sp/ 1 tblsp low fat margarine
275 ml/½ pt skimmed milk
2 size 3 eggs
1 × 2.5 ml sp/½ tsp cinnamon
liquid sweetener to taste
75 g/3 oz wholemeal breadcrumbs ⎫
25 g/1 oz hazelnuts, chopped ⎬ mixed
　　　　　　　　　　　　　　　　⎭

Peel, core and slice the apples. Place in a greased ovenproof dish. Dot with the margarine, then cook for 20-25 minutes at No 2/150°C/ 300°F until apples are barely tender. Whisk milk, eggs, cinnamon and liquid sweetener. Add half the crumb mixture to the liquid and pour over apples. Bake for 25-30 minutes until set. Mix fructose with the remaining breadcrumb mixture. Sprinkle over the pudding and bake until crispy in texture and medium brown in colour.

Serves 4

*Illustrated

80g CHO ⎫
720 Calories ⎬ total

Apple Sponge

2 eating apples
lemon juice
50 g/2 oz wholemeal flour
1 × 5 ml sp/1 tsp baking powder
1 × 2.5 ml sp/½ tsp cinnamon
2 × 15 ml sp/2 tblsp skimmed milk
2 eggs, separated
50 g/2 oz fructose

Wash, core and chop apples. Cover with a little water and lemon juice. Mix flour, baking powder and cinnamon. Gently heat the milk. Whisk egg yolks and fructose until light in colour and thick. Fold in flour mixture and carefully stir in the milk. Finally fold in the stiffly whisked egg whites and the drained apples. Pour mixture into a lightly greased small dish and bake at No 5/190°C/375°F for about 30 minutes or until well risen and golden brown.

Serves 4

60g CHO
600 Calories } **total**

Bread & Butter Pudding

A variation of a traditional pudding.

4 large thin slices wholemeal bread
a little low fat margarine
25 g/1 oz sultanas
100 g/4 oz cooking apple, grated
rind of 1 small lemon, grated (optional)
50 g/2 oz flaked almonds
550 ml/1 pt skimmed milk
2 large eggs
ground nutmeg
liquid sweetener to taste

Thinly spread margarine on the bread, cut each slice into triangles. Mix sultanas, grated apple, lemon rind and half of the almonds. Arrange alternate layers of bread and fruit mixture in a casserole dish with a bread layer on the bottom and top. Add a little liquid sweetener to milk, beat in eggs. Pour over bread ensuring that top slices are moistened. Sprinkle top with remaining almonds and lightly dust with nutmeg. Place dish in a water bath. Bake at No 4/180°C/375°F for 40 minutes, or until liquid is set and the top golden and crispy.

Serves 6

90g CHO
1050 Calories } total

Crunchy Apple Bake

450 g/1 lb prepared cooking apples
1 × 15 ml sp/1 tblsp water
liquid sweetener to taste
1 × 5 ml sp/1 tsp mixed spice *or* **cinnamon**

Topping:
6 large digestive biscuits
50 g/2 oz wheatflakes
50 g/2 oz walnuts, chopped
25 g/1 oz desiccated coconut
rind of 1 orange, grated
25 g/1 oz low fat margarine

Cook apples in water for 5-10 minutes until almost soft. Add spice and sweeten to taste. Turn into an ovenproof dish. Crush the biscuits and combine with wheatflakes, walnuts, coconut and orange rind. Add the margarine and mix thoroughly, then spoon over the apples. Cook at No 4/180°C/350°F for 20 minutes. Serve with yoghurt or an egg based custard.

Serves 4

140g CHO } **total**
1200 Calories

Nutty Orange Mould

75 g/3 oz brown rice
550 ml/1 pt skimmed milk
2 × 5 ml sp/2 tsp wholemeal flour
2 × 15 ml sp/2 tblsp water
1 packet gelatine
1 orange
100 g/4 oz mixed nuts, chopped
liquid sweetener to taste

Bring rice and milk to the boil and simmer for 30 minutes, stirring occasionally to prevent sticking. Mix flour to a smooth paste and stir into the rice mixture and cook for a further 2-3 minutes stirring all the time. Leave to cool. Sweeten to taste. Dissolve the gelatine in a little water, over a low heat. Add the orange juice and rind then beat into the rice with the nuts and chopped orange flesh. Pour into a mould and leave in a cool place to set.

Serves 4

100g CHO
1000 Calories } total

Rhubarb Crumble

450 g/1 lb prepared rhubarb
1 × 5 ml sp/1 tsp cinnamon
liquid sweetener to taste

Crumble:
50 g/2 oz low fat margarine
100 g/4 oz wholemeal flour
25 g/1 oz branflakes

Place rhubarb in an ovenproof dish, add sweetener and cinnamon. Rub fat into the flour until it resembles fine breadcrumbs, then mix in the branflakes. Sprinkle the crumble on the rhubarb. Bake at No 5/190°C/375°F for 40 minutes or until golden brown.

Serves 4

80g CHO
600 Calories } **total**

Light Desserts

This section has a selection of quick and easy light desserts which the whole family will enjoy. Liquid sweetener to taste has been advised in the recipes as this is an ideal way of sweetening products without increasing their calorie or carbohydrate values. Examples of liquid sweeteners are: Hermesetas Liquid, Sweetex Liquid, Natrena Liquid.
When adapting your own recipes remember to add sweetener only after boiling. If sweetener is boiled it tastes bitter. Add a little at a time as 1 × 5 ml sp/1 teaspoon is equivalent in sweetness to 50 g/2 oz sugar.

(left) Strawberry Water Ice, Blackcurrant Fool, Mandarin Surprise

Apple Mousse

1 packet gelatine
2 × 15 ml sp/2 tblsp water
450 g/1 lb prepared cooking apples
150 g/5 fl oz yoghurt (small pot)
2 egg whites
liquid sweetener to taste

Dissolve gelatine in water over a gentle heat. Cook and purée apples. When cool mix in yoghurt and sweetener to taste. Fold the gelatine into the apple mix and when on the point of setting, fold in the stiffly whisked egg whites. Pour into a serving dish and leave to set.

Serves 6

60g CHO
240 Calories } **total**

Blackcurrant Fool

225 g/8 oz blackcurrants, frozen or fresh
liquid sweetener to taste
2 × 15 ml sp/2 tblsp custard powder
275 ml/½ pt skimmed milk
150 g/5 fl oz natural yoghurt (small pot)
50 g/2 oz wheatflakes, slightly crushed
50 g/2 oz hazelnuts, finely chopped

Cook fruit in a little water until soft. Sieve fruit and sweeten to taste. Make custard with custard powder, skimmed milk and sweetener. Add the sieved fruit to the custard. When this mixture is cool, add yoghurt and mix thoroughly. Make layers of fruit, wheatflakes and nuts, finishing with fruit. Decorate the top with wheatflakes and nuts. Place in fridge until required.

*Illustrated

80g CHO
700 Calories } total

Chocolate Mousse

A rich chocolate sweet to be served on special occasions.

100 g/4 oz diabetic chocolate
(fructose sweetened)
4 eggs, separated
4 × 15 ml sp/4 tblsp water
1 × 15 ml sp/1 tblsp rum

Melt chocolate in a basin over hot but not boiling water, add 3 × 15 ml sp/3 tblsp water and stir thoroughly. Add the remaining 15 ml sp/1 tblsp water to the yolks and beat until light in colour. Fold this into the chocolate mixture and remove from heat. Add rum and leave to cool. Whisk egg whites until stiff, then fold carefully into the chocolate mixture. Pour into individual glasses or a soufflé dish. This can be stored in the refrigerator for several hours.

Serves 8

neg CHO
900 Calories } **total**

Fruit Yoghurt Jelly

1 packet gelatine
150 g/5 fl oz blackcurrant yoghurt (small pot)
150 ml/¼ pt skimmed milk
75 ml/⅛ pt sugar-free blackcurrant cordial
150 ml/¼ pt water

30g CHO
210 Calories } total

Grapefruit Meringue

350 g/12 oz blackberries, fresh, frozen
    or canned without sugar
4 grapefruit
liquid sweetener to taste
2 egg whites
2 × 15 ml sp/2 tblsp fructose
2 × 15 ml sp/2 tblsp hazelnuts, chopped

Cut top off each grapefruit, scoop out flesh, remove the core, pith and seeds. Chop flesh and mix with blackberries and liquid sweetener. Fill grapefruits with the mixture and chill for 20 minutes. Beat egg white until thick, then stir in fructose. Pile on top of the grapefruits, sprinkle with nuts and bake at No 5/190°C/375°F for 5 minutes or until browned.

Serves 4

10g CHO
90 Calories } each

Lemon Flan

Base:
25 g/1 oz butter or margarine
1 × 5 ml sp/1 tsp clear honey or treacle
25 g/1 oz ground almonds
50 g/2 oz wheatflakes

Filling:
1 packet gelatine
2 × 15 ml sp/2 tblsp water
2 eggs, separated
1 large lemon (rind and juice)
50 g/2 oz raisins
150 g/5 fl oz natural yoghurt (small pot)
liquid sweetener to taste

Melt fat and honey or treacle together, add almonds and wheatflakes. Press into a 18 cm/ 7" flan ring or spring-sided tin. Leave in the fridge to harden. Dissolve gelatine in water over a gentle heat. Whisk egg yolks with lemon rind until thick and pale in colour. Carefully stir in lemon juice, raisins, yoghurt, liquid sweetener and the slightly cooled gelatine. When the lemon mixture is on the point of setting, fold in whisked egg whites. Pour into the prepared flan ring and leave to set in the fridge.

Serves 6

80g CHO
840 Calories } total

Mandarin Surprise

75 g/3 oz low fat margarine
100 g/4 oz wholemeal flour
50 g/2 oz plain flour
pinch of salt
1 packet gelatine
298 g/10½ oz can mandarins in natural juice
300 g/10 fl oz natural yoghurt (2 small pots)

Rub fat into flour and salt until like fine breadcrumbs. Add enough cold water to form a soft dough. Roll out thinly and line a 20 cm/8″ fluted flan ring. Bake blind for 20 minutes at No 6/200°C/400°F or until crisp. Drain mandarins and reserve juice.
Dissolve gelatine in a little water over a gentle heat. Add reserved juice and whisk into yoghurt. Arrange mandarin segments in the flan case, pour over the cooled yoghurt mixture, leave to set. Decorate with a few reserved mandarin segments.

Serves 6

150g CHO
960 Calories } total

Illustrated

Orange Dessert

2 large oranges
300 g/10 fl oz orange yoghurt (2 small pots)
100 g/4 oz nuts, chopped and toasted

Cut oranges in half, carefully remove segments and place in a large bowl. Clean out each half to leave hollow shell. Mix yoghurt with orange segments. Add half the nuts and fill each shell with the mixture. Sprinkle remaining nuts on top.

Serves 4

15g CHO
225 Calories } each

Pineapple Jelly

1 packet gelatine
275 ml/½ pt unsweetened pineapple juice
150 ml/¼ pt water
liquid sweetener to taste
juice of 1 lemon

Dissolve the gelatine in a little water over a gentle heat. Add pineapple juice, water, sweetener and lemon juice. Pour into dish and leave to set in a cool place. Serve decorated with fruit of choice.

Serves 4

40g CHO
150 Calories } **total**

Strawberry Ice

225 g/8 oz strawberries (fresh or frozen without sugar or syrup)
2 × 15 ml sp/2 tblsp lemon juice
2 × 5 ml sp/2 tsp fructose

Gently cook strawberries in a saucepan. Purée or liquidise the strawberries, add fructose and lemon juice, mix well. Pour into a dish which is suitable to go into a deep freeze. Freeze until half frozen or firm around the edges. Beat well and return to the freezer tray and freeze until firm.

Illustrated

15g CHO
100 Calories } **total**

Cakes, Biscuits & Breads

These recipes concentrate on using high fibre ingredients. The recipes are not significantly lower in fat or calorie content as low fat margarine can not always be used.
What is important is that the quality of carbohydrate is better than if refined ingredients are used.
The difference in taste and texture makes a delicious alternative to conventional cakes, biscuits and breads.

(right) Banana Bread, Oat & Nut Fingers, Wholemeal Rolls

Banana Bread

75 g/3 oz low fat margarine
50 g/2 oz fructose
1 large egg, beaten
275 g/10 oz peeled bananas, mashed
50 g/2 oz walnuts, coarsely chopped
25 g/1 oz hazelnuts, coarsely chopped
225 g/8 oz self-raising wholemeal flour
1 × 5 ml sp/1 tsp baking powder
1 × 2.5 ml sp/½ tsp salt

Cream margarine and fructose until light and fluffy. Gradually add egg, beating well after each addition. Add mashed bananas and nuts and mix well. Fold in flour, salt, baking powder and stir gently. Place in well-greased loaf tin. Bake at No 4/180°C/350°F for 1 — 1¼ hours or until golden and springy to touch.

200g CHO } total
1850 Calories

*Illustrated

Oat & Nut Fingers

Walnuts and almonds have been used here but any chopped nuts will do.

225 g/8 oz rolled oats
25 g/1 oz almonds, chopped
25 g/1 oz walnuts, chopped
50 g/2 oz fructose
150 g/5 oz butter or margarine

Mix all the dry ingredients together in a bowl. Melt the butter or margarine in a pan, add the dry ingredient mixture and mix well. Place this mixture in a swiss roll tin and press down firmly with a fork. Cook at No 4/180°C/350°F for 20-30 minutes or until golden brown in colour. Mark out fingers before it has cooled. When cold cut 16 fingers and remove from tin.

Illustrated

10g CHO
150 Calories } **each**

Shortbread

175 g/6 oz wholemeal flour
25 g/1 oz wholewheat semolina
75 g/3 oz fructose
100 g/4 oz margarine
1 × 2.5 ml sp/½ tsp salt
4 drops vanilla or almond essence

Mix flour, semolina, fructose and salt together. Rub in margarine and add essence. Knead well. Rest for 30 minutes. Shape into a 20 cm/8" round. (Alternatively form into 15 individual fingers). Transfer to a greased or non-stick baking sheet. Bake at No 3/160°C/325°F for approximately 20-25 minutes or until golden brown. Mark into 15 pieces while still hot. If using the finger shape, check after 15 minutes, as they may take a shorter time to cook.

10g CHO
110 Calories } each

Wheaten Fruit Cake

100 g/4 oz wholemeal flour
50 g/2 oz white self-raising flour
50 g/2 oz ground almonds
50 g/2 oz flaked almonds
50 g/2 oz walnuts, roughly chopped
50 g/2 oz Allbran
50 g/2 oz sultanas
25 g/1 oz raisins
25 g/1 oz currants
50 g/2 oz fructose
75 g/3 oz butter or soft margarine
2 large eggs
1 × 5 ml sp/1 tsp gravy browning
1 measure brandy (optional)
1 × 2.5 ml sp/½ tsp salt
2 × 15 ml sp/2 tblsp skimmed milk
3 drops rum essence
1 pinch of nutmeg

Mix dried fruit and add brandy. Leave to stand. Sift flour, salt, nutmeg and add fructose. Rub in butter or margarine, add ground almonds, chopped nuts, Allbran and dried fruit. Mix well. Beat eggs, gravy browning, rum essence and milk together. Add to mixture. Turn into 18 cm/7" non-stick cake tin and bake at No 4/180°C/350°F for approximately 40 minutes. If browning before completely cooked, cover with greaseproof paper and continue cooking until ready. Cool on a wire-rack.
Optional garnish: Glaze with a sugar-free apricot jam and a few glacé cherries.

200g CHO
2260 Calories } total

Wholemeal Rolls

250 g/9 oz wholemeal flour
1 × 2.5 ml sp/½ tsp sugar
15 g/½ oz yeast
150 ml/¼ pt warm water
1 × 2.5 ml sp/½ tsp salt
25 g/1 oz low fat margarine

Cream sugar with yeast and blend with the water. Combine the flour and salt and rub in the margarine. Make a well in the centre and add yeast liquid. Mix thoroughly adding a little extra water if necessary and knead for 5 minutes. Cover with a greased polythene sheet and leave to rise until doubled in size. Knead for 5 minutes. Divide into 8 equal sections and shape. Put on a floured baking tray and glaze with milk. Re-cover and leave to rise until spongy to the touch. Bake for 10 minutes in hot oven at No 7/220°C/425°F until the base of the rolls sound hollow when tapped. Transfer rolls to a wire cooling rack.

Makes 8

**20g CHO
110 Calories** } each

Food Values

Foods	Amount	CHO (approx)	Calories (approx)
Allbran	25 g / 1 oz	12	65
Almonds, *flaked*	25 g / 1 oz	neg	140
Apples, *cooking, prepared*	450 g / 1 lb	42	165
Apples, *eating*	450 g / 1 lb	40	160
Apricots, *1 can in natural juice*	283 g / 10 oz	34	115
Aubergine, *fresh, whole*	450 g / 1 lb	12	50
Bacon, *lean, middle cut, raw*	450 g / 1 lb	—	1900
Bacon, *streaky, raw*	450 g / 1 lb	—	1850
Bananas, *1 small, peeled*	50 g / 2 oz	10	40
Barley, *pearl, raw*	25 g / 1 oz	21	90
Beans, *baked in tomato sauce*	75 g / 3 oz	10	55
Beans, *broad, fresh, frozen*	25 g / 1 oz	2	15
Beans, *butter, canned*	1 large can	55	300
	1 small can	30	180
Beans, *butter, dried*	25 g / 1 oz	12	65
Beans, *haricot, canned*	1 large can	55	300
	1 small can	30	180
Beans, *haricot, dried*	25 g / 1 oz	11	60
Beans, *kidney, canned*	1 large can	60	330
	1 small can	30	165
Beans, *kidney, dried*	25 g / 1 oz	11	70
Beans, *runner, frozen*	25 g / 1 oz	neg	5
Bean sprouts	100 g / 4 oz	neg	10
Beef, *lean, raw, braising steak*	450 g / 1 lb	—	900
Beef, *lean, raw, minced*	450 g / 1 lb	—	1000
Beef, *lean, raw, stewing steak*	450 g / 1 lb	—	900
Blackberries	175 g / 6 oz	10	50
Blackcurrants	225 g / 8 oz	15	60
Branflakes, *breakfast cereal*	25 g / 1 oz	17	80
Brazil Nuts, *shelled*	25 g / 1 oz	neg	150
Bread, *brown mix*	283 g / 10 oz	170	850
Bread, *wholemeal, large loaf*	1 slice	15	65
Breadcrumbs, *wholemeal, fresh*	25 g / 1 oz	10	55
Cabbage, *fresh, raw*	450 g / 1 lb	15	100
Carrots, *fresh, raw*	450 g / 1 lb	25	100
Cashew nuts, *shelled*	25 g / 1 oz	4	195
Cauliflower, *fresh, raw*	450 g / 1 lb	5	60
Celery	450 g / 1 lb	5	40
Cheese, *Cheddar*	25 g / 1 oz	—	100-120
Cheese, *cottage*	100 g / 4 oz	—	100
Cheese, *cream*	100 g / 4 oz	—	440
Cheese, *Edam*	25 g / 1 oz	—	75
Cheese, *Parmesan*	25 g / 1 oz	—	100
Chicken, *breast, raw*	100 g / 4 oz	—	115

Food Values

Foods	Amount	CHO (approx)	Calories (approx)
Chicken, *cooked*	100 g/4 oz	—	150
Chicken, *1 drumstick, raw*	100 g/4 oz	—	80
Chicken, *1 large leg, raw*	225 g/8 oz	—	200
Chick-peas, *canned*	1 large can	60	300
	1 small can	30	150
Chick-peas, *dried*	25 g/1 oz	12	80
Cod steak, *frozen*	100 g/4 oz	—	80
Corned Beef, *canned*	100 g/4 oz	—	200
Cornflour	1 × 15 ml sp/ 1 tblsp	15	55
Courgettes, *fresh, raw*	450 g/1 lb	15	70
Cucumber, *fresh, large*	225 g/8 oz	neg	20
Currants, *dried*	25 g/1 oz	15	60
Custard Powder	1 × 15 ml sp/ 1 tblsp	15	55
Coconut, *dried*	25 g/1 oz	neg	150
Digestive Biscuits, *1 large*	15 g/½ oz	10	70
Egg, *1 standard*		—	80
Egg, *1 white*		—	5
Egg, *1 yolk*		—	75
Flour, *white, plain*	25 g/1 oz	20	88

Foods	Amount	CHO (approx)	Calories (approx)
Flour, *white, self-raising*	25 g/1 oz	19	85
Flour, *wholemeal*	25 g/1 oz	16	80
Frankfurter, *10 tinned in brine*	225 g/8 oz	15	550
Fructose	25 g/1 oz	*	100
Garlic Sausage	100 g/4 oz	—	450
Grapefruit, *1 large*	225 g/8 oz	10	50
Grapes, *fresh*	100 g/4 oz	15	60
Haddock, *smoked*	450 g/1 lb	—	360
Ham, *cooked*	100 g/4 oz	—	120
Hazelnuts, *shelled*	25 g/1 oz	neg	95
Herrings, *1 filletted*	100 g/4 oz	—	140
Honey	1 × 5 ml sp/ 1 tsp	4	15
Kidney, *lamb's*	225 g/8 oz	—	200
Lamb, *breast of*	1 medium	—	1500
Lamb, *cooked*	450 g/1 lb	—	900
Leek, *fresh, raw*	450 g/1 lb	25	135
Lemon, *1*	50 g/2 oz	neg	8-10
Lentils, *dried, raw*	100 g/4 oz	50	300

*Not counted, but maximum intake 50 g/2 ozs a day

Food Values

Foods	Amount	CHO (approx)	Calories (approx)
Liver, *chicken, raw*	100 g/4 oz	—	135
Liver, *lamb's, raw*	100 g/4 oz	—	180
Liver, *pig's, raw*	100 g/4 oz	—	155
Mackerel, *fillets*	450 g/1 lb	—	800
Mackerel, *whole*	450 g/1 lb	—	450
Mandarins, *1 can in natural juice*	298 g/10½ oz	24	80
Margarine	25 g/1 oz	—	180
Margarine, *low fat*	25 g/1 oz	—	90
Mayonnaise	1 × 15 ml sp/ 1 tblsp	—	100
Milk	550 ml/1 pt	27-30	360
Milk, *skimmed, fresh*	550 ml/1 pt	27-30	180
Millet, *ground*	25 g/1 oz	18	60
Mixed Vegetables, *frozen*	100 g/4 oz	10	60
Mushrooms, *raw*	100 g/4 oz	neg	15
Nuts, *mixed*	25 g/1 oz	neg	130
Oats, *rolled, porridge*	25 g/1 oz	18	100
Oil, *vegetable*	1 × 15 ml sp/ 1 tblsp	—	135
Onions, *1 large, raw*	225 g/8 oz	10	50
Orange, *1 large, fresh*	150 g/5 oz	10	40
Orange juice, *1 carton, unsweetened*	1000 ml (1 litre) 1¾ pts	85-100	350
Parsnips, *1 small*	225 g/8 oz	18	80
Pasta, *wholewheat lasagne, macaroni shells, spaghetti*	100 g/4 oz	65	325
Peanuts	25 g/1 oz	2	140
Peanuts, *dry, roasted*	25 g/1 oz	3	135
Peas, *frozen, cooked*	25 g/1 oz	neg	10
Peas, *yellow, split, dried*	25 g/1 oz	12	70
Peppers, *1 medium fresh, red, green*	100 g/4 oz	neg	15
Pilchards, *1 can, in tomato sauce*	425 g/15 oz	—	675
Pineapple, *1 can in natural juice*	225 g/8 oz	37	135
Pineapple Juice, *1 carton, unsweetened*	1000 ml (1 litre) 1¾ pts	135	550
Pork, *mince, raw*	450 g/1 lb	—	750
Pork, *lean, raw*	450 g/1 lb	—	700
Potato, *unpeeled*	450 g/1 lb	80	340
prepared ie peeled	450 g/1 lb	95	400
Prawns, *fresh or frozen*	100 g/4 oz	—	100

Food Values

Foods	Amount	CHO (approx)	Calories (approx)
Raisins, *dried*	25 g / 1 oz	16	60
Rhubarb, *uncooked, prepared*	450 g / 1 lb	5	25
Rice, *brown, raw*	100 g / 4 oz	80	350
Salami, *sliced*	100 g / 4 oz	—	490
Sausages, *pork, chipolatas*	2	5	180-200
Sausages, *pork*	1	5	180-200
Sausage Meat, *pork*	450 g / 1 lb	55	1440
Semolina, *wholewheat*	100 g / 4 oz	70	330
Shredded Wheat	1	18	80
Soya Beans, *dried*	25 g / 1 oz	7	100
Soya Mince, *before reconstitution*	100 g / 4 oz	15 max	250
Strawberries, *fresh, prepared*	450 g / 1 lb	28	120
Suet, *shredded*	25 g / 1 oz	3	205
Sultanas, *dried*	25 g / 1 oz	16	60
Sweetcorn, *canned*	25 g / 1 oz	4	20
Sweetcorn, *frozen*	25 g / 1 oz	6	30
Tomatoes, *1 large can*	400 g / 14 oz	8	50
Tomatoes, *fresh*	450 g / 1 lb	12	65
Tomato Juice, *1 carton, unsweetened*	1000 ml (1 litre) / 1¾ pts	35	160

Foods	Amount	CHO (approx)	Calories (approx)
Tomato Purée	1 × 15 ml sp / 1 tblsp	neg	10
Treacle	1 × 5 ml sp / 1 tsp	4	65
Tuna, *1 can, in brine*	185 g / 6½ oz	neg	200
Turkey, *cooked*	100 g / 4 oz	—	130
Veal, *lean*	450 g / 1 lb	—	440
Walnuts	25 g / 1 oz	neg	130
Weetabix	1	12	60
Wheatflakes, *breakfast cereal*	25 g / 1 oz	17	85
Wheatgerm	25 g / 1 oz	10	85
Wholewheat grains	25 g / 1 oz	17	85
Wine, *white, dry*	150 ml / ¼ pt	neg	100
Yoghurt, *1 small pot* blackcurrant	150 g / 5 fl oz	20-25	150
Yoghurt, *1 small pot natural*	150 g / 5 fl oz	10-15	50-70
Yoghurt, *1 small pot orange*	150 g / 5 fl oz	20-25	150
Yoghurt, *1 large pot natural*	450 g / 20 fl oz	30-45	150-200

Index

199

201

202

205